THE
VICTORIAN
TREASURY

THE
VICTORIAN
TREASURY

A collection of fascinating facts and insights
about the Victorian Era

Lucinda Hawksley

ANDRE
DEUTSCH

For Helena and James

THIS IS AN ANDRE DEUTSCH BOOK

Published in 2015 by André Deutsch Limited
a division of the Carlton Publishing Group
20 Mortimer Street
London W1T 3JW

10 9 8 7 6 5 4 3 2 1

A catalogue record for this book is available from the British Library

ISBN 978 0 233 00477 8

Printed in Dubai

CONTENTS

INTRODUCTION

When Queen Victoria came to the throne in 1837, it heralded a fresh start for the British Isles. The arrival of a new young queen – who was barely 18 years old when she was pronounced monarch – was a welcome change after what had been a very difficult, dissolute and often debauched time for the British monarchy. For decades, Britain had been ruled by a succession of German kings from the House of Hanover, beginning with King George I, who had spoken almost no English and professed an utter lack of interest in learning anything about his new kingdom.

By the time of Queen Victoria, the older generation of her subjects could still remember the so-called "madness" of King George III, who had been succeeded by two of his most scandalous sons: King George IV (who had served as prince regent during the latter years of his father's reign and illness) and King William IV. By the 1830s, the British public had been growing increasingly angry with Hanoverian kings, and the succession of a very young queen was a welcome relief from the generations of corpulent, decadent monarchs. At the start and again by the end of her reign, the Queen was popular, but for several decades she was as unpopular as her uncles and grandfather.

The young Princess Victoria's childhood had been sheltered, and she had lived in relative obscurity with her widowed mother, the Duchess of Kent, at Kensington Palace. Her father, Prince Edward, the Duke of Kent and Strathearn (another son of King George III), had died when she was a baby. As the Duchess of Kent was German, her fatherless daughter grew up speaking German. In Victoria's early life, few people even considered that she might one day become queen – even though King George IV's only legitimate child, Princess Charlotte, had died while giving birth to her son in 1817 (two years before Princess Victoria was born).

King George IV had no more legitimate children and his brother, the future King William IV, fared no better. All of William's legitimate heirs with his wife, Queen Adelaide, died in infancy. However, the general public knew that he had several healthy illegitimate children with his mistress of many years, the actress known as Mrs Jordan.

Princess Victoria was already into her teens before the newspapers and the public began to pay much attention to her as a possible queen-in-waiting. She was declared queen on the death of King William IV, a month after her eighteenth birthday. The king had been desperate to stay alive until his niece reached 18, the age at which she could inherit the throne without the need for another regency. The period of time now known to historians as the Victorian Age began with the date on which the princess was told of her uncle's death – 20 June 1837 – and ended with Queen Victoria's death on 22 January 1901.

The Victorian Age was one of the greatest times of change that Britain had ever experienced in terms of technology, social upheaval and political metamorphosis. It was the first time that the country had been ruled by a female monarch since the brief reign of Queen Anne, who had died in 1714. Ironically, though, the social welfare and legal position of women in Britain changed remarkably little during the reign of Victoria, compared to that of men.

Under Queen Victoria, Britain became one of the most powerful countries in the world, thanks to the ever-expanding British Empire. However, Victoria's reign also had political repercussions that would be felt long after her death, such as setting in motion the chain of events that would lead to the First World War.

In the mid-1830s, the population of Great Britain was just over 16 million people; by the end of Queen Victoria's reign, in 1901, that had increased to approximately 37 million. This enormous growth in population was due partly to improvements in the medical industry as well as to breakthroughs made in scientific research and improvements in housing, healthcare, hygiene and sanitation.

It was also due to the regular arrival of migrants from all over the British Empire. But despite such massive growth in the British population, there were also many Britons who left the country, particularly those from the poorest sections of society, desperate for a better quality of life in the New World. It is estimated that around 19 million people left Britain to live overseas in the century leading up to the First World War. Many of them were embracing the spirit of adventure that new and better forms of transport made possible for the first time. This mass migration resulted in huge new British populations in the Americas, Australia and New Zealand in particular.

The landscape of Great Britain was changed forever by the Industrial Revolution; as a result of mining, factories and the railways, the country was transformed from a predominantly agricultural land to a country of manufacturers. Britain was no longer a predominantly rural culture, and embraced its urban sprawl and the growth of suburbia.

1

QUEEN VICTORIA AND THE ROYAL FAMILY

At the start of Queen Victoria's reign, the British government was well aware that the public interest in, and affection for, the royal family had been waning steadily over recent decades. The antics of the Hanoverian kings had sorely tested the public, and a new type of royal was needed to avoid the kind of revolutions that were starting to foment all over Europe.

VICTORIA AND ALBERT

In 1836, the teenaged Princess Victoria had been taken to meet two of her German cousins, Prince Ernst and Prince Albert of Saxe-Coburg and Gotha. It was hoped by the Duchess of Kent that her daughter would marry Ernst, the older brother, but Victoria was immediately attracted to the more retiring, younger Albert, who was the same age as she. After she became queen, Victoria proposed to Albert – because he was now of a lower rank, protocol dictated that he could not propose to a queen. The engagement was not only a love match, which was highly unusual for a royal marriage; it was also a great way of renewing the public's interest in their monarch.

A royal wedding was exactly the kind of good publicity that the British monarchy needed. It took place amid much national excitement on 10 February 1840, at St James's Palace in London, and was the first time since 1554 that the wedding of an already reigning queen had taken place in England.

VICTORIA AND ALBERT'S WEDDING FACTS

- The wedding took place at the Chapel Royal at St James's Palace in London. The ceremony was performed by the Archbishop of Canterbury.
- The start of the day did not bode well as it rained copiously in the morning. Despite this, huge crowds of people turned out to watch the occasion.
- The procession began at midday at Buckingham Palace, where the army fired a 21-gun salute.
- There were 12 bridesmaids.
- Queen Victoria wore a dress of white satin (made by seamstresses in Spitalfields, East London), trimmed with lace orange-flower blossoms and Honiton lace.
- The lace used for the wedding dress alone cost £1,000. It was made in the village of Beer, Devon, a few miles from Honiton; more than 200 lace makers had worked on it for eight months.
- The veil was also made of Honiton lace, and took six weeks to create. It was held in place with a wreath of orange-flower blossoms.
- Much was made of how much work the Queen's wedding outfit had given to "poor weavers".
- The wedding dress began a new fashion of getting married in white.
- Prince Albert wore the uniform of a field marshal, but with rosettes of white satin on his shoulders (to match Victoria's dress).
- The wedding cake weighed around 300 lb (136 kg) and had a circumference of 9 ft (2.7 m).

Upon the royal couple's marriage, Albert became known as the Prince Consort; the Queen tried to have him created king and her co-monarch, but Parliament steadfastly refused. Kings were more powerful than queens, and the government had no intention of allowing a foreign prince to be heralded as the more powerful partner than a British-born queen.

The marriage between Queen Victoria and Prince Albert is traditionally seen as a great love story. It was, but it was also a very turbulent union of two extremely forceful personalities – the couple's arguments became legendary among the royal servants. The marriage was also a very sexual relationship, contrary to perceived notions about the Victorian era. The Queen recorded her most intimate memories in her diaries (these were heavily edited after her death by her youngest daughter, Princess Beatrice).

Queen Victoria fell pregnant immediately after her wedding day, and the couple's eldest child, a daughter named Victoria (but known as Vicky to distinguish her from her mother), was born at Buckingham Palace on 21 November 1840. Princess Vicky was to be the eldest of nine children – five girls and four boys – all of whom survived infancy, which was unusual at this time of high infant mortality.

Queen Victoria has become notorious for her dislike of babies, even her own. She found pregnancy debilitating, childbirth horrifying, and babies themselves to be "ugly", disgusting little creatures whose very way of moving revolted her. She wrote of how much she disliked the jerky way in which babies moved, describing it as "that terrible froglike action". It is not surprising that the eight eldest children keenly felt the lack of interest or love from their mother, whose affections seemed to be entirely wrapped up in her husband. The princes were also scared of Prince Albert, who was a great believer in physical punishment for his sons – although he seems to have been much gentler towards the princesses.

It was only the last royal child, Princess Beatrice, who seemed to arouse maternal emotions in the Queen, and as a result the royal servants and Beatrice's siblings found her spoilt and rude. As a small child, Beatrice was allowed to behave as she liked without being told off by her mother, but sadly this had repercussions for her adult life, when her siblings still resented and disliked her because of their mother's favouritism. At the very start of his reign, immediately after Queen Victoria's death, King Edward VII began to take back from his youngest sister most of the property their mother had given her. Even at the age of 59, he was still angry about their childhood.

In 1861, the Queen and her children were devastated and the whole country shocked by the death of Prince Albert. The Prince Consort was believed to have died of typhoid fever, after having been suffering from a variety of recurring symptoms for several months. In recent years, medical historians have disputed the Victorian diagnosis of typhoid, suggesting that it may have been Crohn's disease or some type of cancer that killed the Prince Consort, but at the time of his death the medical experts were convinced it was typhoid. Newspapers around the British Empire recorded Prince Albert's death in articles inspired by the public fashion for ostentatious mourning – a fashion that would grow even more pronounced when the Queen continued to wear her widow's costume for the next four decades. In late 1861, the Irish press ran the following article, in the flowery language favoured by Victorian journalism:

> *Death has snatched another victim, and this time the Husband of our beloved Queen. The British Nation feels deeply the loss sustained in this bereavement, not so much on its own sake – though that will be deeply felt – as looking on this loss their deeply respected Queen has sustained in losing one of the best of Husbands. For upwards of twenty-two years his late Royal Highness has occupied the exalted position of Husband to Queen Victoria of England; and during that protracted period, he has invariably shown his qualifications for his position, as a good Husband, an exemplary Father, and a sage Councillor. During his connection with this Country, Prince Albert worthily earned "golden opinions" for himself, by his talents, his urbanity, his perseverance, and, without unduly obtruding himself on public notice, he was a wise Councillor to Her Majesty, a good and supporting Husband to his Royal Wife, and a proper Father to his Royal Children! His death – at so early an age – is a striking exemplification of the frailty of human life, but he has departed, leaving behind him the proper path to be walked by a good Husband and a good Father!*
>
> **The Waterford Chronicle**, 20 December 1861

ASSASSINATION ATTEMPTS

During her reign, seven attempts were made on Queen Victoria's life. On one occasion, a gunman leapt onto the carriage she was travelling in; he was felled by a quick punch from John Brown, the Queen's Highland ghillie (servant).

VICTORIA REGINA

The letters "V.R." symbolize much of Queen Victoria's reign and can be seen on pillar boxes, architecture and official papers. They stand for Victoria Regina – *regina* being the Latin word for "queen". After 1887, this monogram was often changed to "V.R.I.": Victoria Regina Imperatrix (which means "empress"), to reflect her new position as Empress of India.

THE ROYAL CHILDREN

Princess Victoria Adelaide Mary Louise (1840–1901), the Princess Royal, was known in the family as Vicky. A highly intelligent child, she was considered something of a prodigy by her teachers; she was also a talented artist. At the age of 15 she fell in love with Frederick, the future Emperor of Prussia, whom she called Fritz. The Queen considered her too young to have her engagement announced publicly, but when it was made public knowledge, the country had mixed feelings – many were unhappy that their pretty Princess Royal was to leave the country. Vicky and Fritz married in 1858; although it was a love match, however, her life in Prussia was deeply unhappy. She had a good relationship with her husband, but not with the rest of the court, who disliked and distrusted her solely for being English (even though her father was German and her mother half-German). Vicky and Fritz's eldest son, Wilhelm, had a disabled arm, caused by his very difficult birth, in which the Prussian doctors gave up both the mother and baby for dead. It was only thanks to the British doctor sent out by Queen Victoria that they both survived. Wilhelm would eventually succeed his father and become known as Kaiser Wilhelm – he nursed a lifelong grievance against his mother's British relations, especially his uncle Bertie, with whom he shared a mutual dislike. It was Kaiser Wilhelm who led his country against Britain in the First World War. Princess Vicky died of cancer seven months after the death of her mother (whose funeral she had been too ill to attend). She was buried in Potsdam, beside her husband Fritz.

Prince Edward Albert (1841–1910) was known as Bertie. Throughout his childhood, Bertie had no idea that he would one day be king. He didn't know that the law of succession decreed that men inherited at the expense of their sisters – he was enlightened by one of his tutors, who was amazed to discover the boy had never had the fact explained to him. The brilliant Vicky always overshadowed Bertie in the schoolroom and was very protective of him against his bullying parents, who told him repeatedly that he was a disappointment. Throughout his life, Bertie would be made to feel he was never good enough for his mother; the Queen even blamed him for his father's death. Although the doctors told her that Prince Albert had died of typhoid, the Queen insisted that it was his horror at Bertie's behaviour that had killed him: shortly before Albert's final illness they had discovered that Bertie had lost his virginity to an actress named Nellie Clifton, a scandal that made it into the newspapers. In 1863, still scorned by his widowed mother, Bertie married Princess Alexandra, known as Alix, the daughter of the Danish king and queen. Bertie was known as the Prince of Wales until he finally became King Edward VII after the death of his mother, in 1901. Queen Victoria was determined that her son should make her husband's name that of a king and insisted he call himself King Albert. He refused to do so. Despite his mother's dire protestations that Bertie would be a terrible king, King Edward VII was a talented diplomat, helped by his speaking several languages. His scandalous lifestyle did not end with his marriage, and he had numerous affairs. His most famous lovers were Lillie Langtry, Mrs Keppel and the courtesan Catherine Walters, nicknamed "Skittles" – but there were very many more. King Edward VII ruled for only nine years, a time known as the Edwardian period. He died of pneumonia at the age of 68, and was succeeded by his son King George V.

Princess Alice Mary Maud (1843–78) was very close to Bertie, and renowned for being the peacemaker of the family. Throughout Alice's childhood, Queen Victoria wrote repeatedly of her fears that her daughter was "backward", despite the fact that Alice was a strong personality with a curious nature. She became a very adept nurse when her father was dying and kept up her interest in medicine and nursing, much against her mother's wishes, into adulthood. Bertie was devastated when Alice married in 1862 and, like her older sister, moved to Germany. Her husband was Prince Louis of Hesse-Darmstadt and Alice became the Grand Duchess of Hesse-Darmstadt. Their wedding, which took place the year after her father's death, was described as being more like a funeral than a wedding, as the Queen insisted the chapel be swathed in black mourning fabric in memory of Prince Albert. While living in Darmstadt, Alice became a pioneer of the nursing industry. She pushed for proper training for and treatment of professional nurses, and was particularly interested in what was then a sadly neglected sphere of medicine: gynaecology. She died tragically young, after she and her youngest daughter, Mary, contracted diphtheria. Both mother and toddler died of the disease; Alice died on the seventeenth anniversary of her father's death, 14 December 1878. One of Alice and Louis's grandchildren was Princess Alexandra, who married Tsar Nicholas of Russia and was executed with her family in 1917.

Prince Alfred Ernest Albert (1844–1900) was known as "Affie". From a very young age, he wanted to be a sailor and joined the Navy as a teenager. After this, his mother began writing about him very fondly, regularly telling people what a tragedy it was that Bertie had been born before Affie, as the younger prince would make a much better king than his brother. He was given the title of the Duke of Edinburgh and later inherited the duchy of Saxe-Coburg-Gotha following the death of his childless uncle (his father's brother). In 1868, Alfred was in Australia when he was targeted by a Fenian would-be assassin and shot. His attacker, Henry James O'Farrell, shot the prince right through his body, but the bullet somehow missed any vital organs. O'Farrell was hanged within weeks of the attack. In 1874, Alfred married the Grand Duchess Marie, daughter of the Tsar of Russia. It was a deeply unhappy marriage and Alfred became an alcoholic who suffered from severe depression.

Princess Helena Augusta Victoria (1846–1923) was known as "Lenchen" (the German diminutive of her name). Her birth was so difficult that Prince Albert feared both his wife and the baby would die. As a child, Helena was a tomboy, who was said to join in fistfights with her brothers. Her mother considered Helena the least attractive of her daughters – she felt that Helena's face was too long and bemoaned how difficult it would be to find her a husband. Despite her mother's predictions, Helena did marry. Her husband was Prince Christian of Schleswig-Holstein, who was 15 years older than she. Queen Victoria agreed to the marriage on the condition that the couple remained living in England. Helena and Christian had four sons and two daughters, although one son was stillborn and another died within a few days of his birth. Like her sister Alice, Helena took an interest in nursing, and became the patron of a number of charities. She was also a founding member of the British Red Cross. Helena's eldest son, Christian, was killed in the Boer War. Her second son, Albert, inherited family land titles in Prussia and fought for Germany in the First World War. Despite having four adult children, Helena and Christian had only one grandchild (an illegitimate daughter of Prince Albert).

Princess Louise Caroline Alberta (1848–1939) adored her father, who died when Louise was 13, and had a very difficult relationship with her mother. Against Victoria's advice, Louise became a professional sculptor – her mother wanted her to become a painter as she considered sculpting a "masculine" art form. It is rumoured that in her teens Louise had an illegitimate baby, fathered by her brother Leopold's tutor. The baby is said to have been adopted by the son of the Queen's gynaecologist. In 1871, Louise married the Marquis of Lorne, the eldest son of the 8th Duke of Argyll (an heir to the title), who is believed to have been homosexual. Louise became an integral part of the London art scene, gaining her earliest fame during the period of the Aesthetic movement, and had a long-term love affair with her sculpting tutor, Joseph Edgar Boehm. She lived in Canada when her husband was Governor-General (1878–83) and both Lake Louise and the province of Alberta were named after her. She was a fervent supporter of women's rights – in opposition to her mother – and of health and education reform. Louise had no more children, but was adored by her nieces and nephews, and was a passionate supporter of and a tireless fundraiser for children's hospitals as well as other charities. She helped found the Girls' Public Day School Trust and encouraged education for all social classes and both genders. She died just after the beginning of the Second World War at the age of 91.

Prince Arthur William Patrick Albert (1850–1942), also known as the Duke of Connaught and Strathearn, joined the army at the age of 16 (one of his godfathers was the military commander the 1st Duke of Wellington, whose birthday he shared and after whom he was named). He undertook military service all over the world, including Canada, Africa, Europe and India. In 1879, he married Princess Louise of Prussia and they had three children; he also maintained a long-term relationship with the American heiress Leonie, Lady Leslie (née Leonie Jerome), the aunt of Sir Winston Churchill. In 1911, he became Governor-General of Canada for five years. He was also one of the country's most prominent freemasons and a supporter of the new Boy Scout movement, set up by his friend Lord Baden-Powell. After being widowed in 1917, Arthur became less interested in public duties and spent much of his time in seaside towns in England, in the South of France or with his widowed sister, Princess Louise. They both lived to the age of 91.

Prince Leopold George Duncan Albert (1853–84), also known as the Duke of Albany, was a haemophiliac. As such, his childhood was very sheltered and he spent much of his life ill and frustrated that he was unable to lead the exciting, active life led by his brothers. In 1872, he entered Christ Church College, Oxford, where he became friendly with the academic Charles Lutwidge Dodgson (better known as Lewis Carroll) and seems to have fallen in love with the daughter of the Dean; her name was Alice Liddell, and as a child she had been the inspiration for Dodgson's *Alice in Wonderland*. They became good friends. He married Princess Helena of Waldeck-Pyrmont in 1882 and, when they had a daughter in 1883, he asked that they name her Alice. (Alice Liddell named her second son Leopold and asked Prince Leopold to be his godfather.) As a child who was unable to participate in physical sports, Leopold became a fervent chess player and helped promote the game in Britain. He was also a freemason. Leopold and Helena had two children, but he was fated never to meet his youngest child. Following a seemingly minor accident, Leopold suffered a haemorrhage and bled to death. He was 30 years old. His wife gave birth to their son, Prince Charles Edward, four months later.

Princess Beatrice Mary Victoria Feodore (1856–1944) was her mother's favourite child and, as such, often resented by her siblings. During her childhood, she enjoyed being spoilt by her mother, but as an adolescent and adult the relationship became stifling and isolated her from many of her brothers and sisters. Her mother was determined that Beatrice would not marry and leave her. At the age of 28, however, Beatrice was permitted to marry. Her husband was Prince Henry of Battenberg, known as Liko; the media made much of how handsome he was and how plain Beatrice seemed by comparison. It was not an easy marriage and lasted only 13 years, ending when Liko died of malaria on his way to fight in the Ashanti wars in Africa. Like her mother, Beatrice found herself a young widow, aged only 40, and the two women became even closer. She and Liko had four children (three sons and a daughter); their daughter Victoria Eugenie, known as Ena, became Queen of Spain and somehow survived an anarchist's bomb thrown at her carriage on her wedding day. Beatrice's youngest son, Maurice, was killed in action within a few weeks of the start of the First World War.

QUEEN VICTORIA'S LANGUAGES

The queen's first language was German. From the age of three, she also began to learn English and French. In the 1880s, by which time she had been named Empress of India, Victoria began learning Urdu and Hindi. Her teacher was Abdul Karim, known as the *munshi*, which she translated as "teacher".

ABDUL KARIM (1863–1909)

One of Queen Victoria's favourite staff members was Abdul Karim, who first arrived in England in 1887 at the age of 24. The Queen had requested two waiters be hired from India to serve the Indian dignitaries coming to celebrate her Golden Jubilee. The Queen recorded in her journal about the two new staff members: "The one Mohammed Buksh, very dark with a very smiling expression... and the other, much younger, called Abdul Karim, is much lighter, tall and with a fine, serious countenance. His father is a native doctor at Agra. They both kissed my feet."

Queen Victoria took such a fond liking to Abdul Karim that within a short time she had promoted him from waiter to one of her most intimate members of staff. He held great power within the royal court and was disliked by the Queen's children and by many other senior staff members as being her "spy" within the court. As soon as he became king, Edward VII ordered soldiers to enter Abdul Karim's home and seize any papers they could find. Abdul Karim and his family returned to India soon afterwards. Despite the vigilance of the soldiers, one of his diaries was smuggled out of the country and still survives.

QUEEN VICTORIA AND SCOTLAND

Queen Victoria and Prince Albert first visited Scotland in 1842 and vowed to return, as they had both fallen in love with the Scottish Highlands. In 1848, they took the lease on a grand property known as Balmoral, even though they hadn't seen it beforehand. The house was not quite big enough, but they loved its location so, four years later, they bought it. Immediately they set about building a bigger castle on the site, large enough to accommodate all the royal family, their guests and their servants. Queen Victoria laid the foundation stone for the new castle on 28 September 1853 and it was completed in 1856. It became one of the Queen's favourite places (although the royal children hated spending time there as it was so cold and Victoria insisted they all wear Scottish kilts).

The Queen's love of Scotland created a booming new industry in tourism. It made tartan fashionable all over Britain (much to the chagrin of the Scottish) and, more importantly, it helped heal rifts between England and Scotland after years of government suppression. The Queen commissioned new tartans for herself and her family, and Albert was regularly seen wearing his kilt. Had he still been alive, the novelist Sir Walter Scott would have been thrilled to see how rapidly sales of his books rose – novels about Scotland, and the Scottish Highlands in particular, became the latest fashion in reading material.

> *With great ceremony, in accordance with a memorandum drawn up by the Prince for the occasion, the foundation-stone of the new edifice (Balmoral Castle) was laid, and by 1855 it was habitable. Spacious, built of granite in the Scotch baronial style, with a tower 100 feet high, and minor turrets and castellated gables, the castle was skilfully arranged to*

command the finest views of the surrounding mountains and of the neighbouring river Dee. Upon the interior decorations Albert and Victoria lavished all their care. The wall and the floors were of pitch-pine, and covered with specially manufactured tartans. The Balmoral tartan ... and the Victoria tartan ... were to be seen in every room: there were tartan curtains, and tartan chair-covers, and even tartan linoleums. Occasionally the Royal Stuart tartan appeared, for Her Majesty always maintained that she was an ardent Jacobite. Water-colour sketches by Victoria hung upon the walls, together with innumerable stags' antlers, and the head of a boar, which had been shot by Albert in Germany. In an alcove in the hall, stood a life-sized statue of Albert in Highland dress.

Victoria declared that it was perfection. "Every year", she wrote, "my heart becomes more fixed in this dear paradise, and so much more so now, that ALL has become my dear Albert's own creation, own work, own building, own layout... and his great taste, and the impress of his dear hand, have been stamped everywhere."

From **Queen Victoria** by [Giles] Lytton Strachey, 1921

JOHN BROWN (1826–83)

In 1848, John Brown started working for the Queen and Prince Albert. Within a few years he had become Victoria's ghillie, or personal Highland servant. After Prince Albert's death, she became increasingly close to Brown and there were even rumours of a love affair – rumours so widespread that they reached the newspapers. The Queen's children despised Brown, and hated how close he was to their mother.

After John Brown saved her from an assassination attempt in 1872, the Queen showed him even greater favouritism. His brother, Archie Brown, was also given special treatment by Victoria. Despite the fact that Archie was cruel and unkind to the royal children, the Queen made the extraordinary decision to let him look after the sickly young Prince Leopold. The prince hated him and told his siblings that Archie pinched and physically hurt him despite knowing he was haemophiliac. In 1869, the Queen asked the sculptor Joseph Edgar Boehm to create a portrait bust of John Brown; in 1901, after his mother's death, the new King Edward VII ordered that it be smashed.

In the 1880s, a dying clergyman in Scotland told his sister that some years earlier he had performed a marriage ceremony for the Queen and John Brown. More credence is given to this rumour by the Queen's faithful doctor, Sir John Reid. He recorded that he had been instructed to perform certain duties after the Queen's death: he placed in her coffin not only specific items belonging to Prince Albert but also a photograph of John Brown, a lock of his hair, one of his handkerchiefs and Brown's mother's wedding ring (which he had given to the Queen and which she had worn for many years).

After Queen Victoria's death, Princess Beatrice went through all her mother's letters and journals, and deleted anything she considered to be injurious to her mother's reputation – including a huge number of entries about John Brown. A few years after Queen Victoria's death, King Edward VII received blackmail threats from a former manager of the Balmoral estate who, like so many other members of the royal household, had detested Brown. Sir James Reid was sent to bargain with him, and to retrieve around 300 letters. He spent six months negotiating for the letters, which he described in his own journal as "most compromising" – and then burnt them all.

That devil Archie, he does nothing, but jeer at, & be impertinent to me every day, & in the night he won't do anything for me though I order it, not even give me my chamberpot ... the infernal blackguard. I could tear him limb from limb I loathe him so.

Prince Leopold to his friend and tutor Major Collins about
Archie Brown

Brown was a rude, unmannerly fellow ... but he had unbounded influence with the Queen whom he treated with little respect, presuming in every way on his position with her. It was the talk of all the household that he was "The Queen's stallion" – He was a fine man physically, though coarsely made, and had fine eyes (like the late Prince Consort's it was said) and the Queen, who had been passionately in love with her husband ... got it into her head that somehow the Prince's spirit had passed into Brown.

From the journals of Wilfrid Scawen Blunt (1840–1922)

⤨ During Queen Victoria's reign, London was the largest city in the world.

⤨ Queen Victoria was the first monarch to make Buckingham Palace her London home; until then it was known as Buckingham House.

⤨ Queen Victoria reigned for 63 years, seven months and two days.

THE QUEEN'S FAVOURITE RESIDENCES

- Buckingham Palace in London

- Windsor Castle in Berkshire

- Balmoral in the Scottish Highlands

- Osborne House on the Isle of Wight (which Prince Albert adored because he said the view reminded him of the Bay of Naples)

- Holyrood House in Edinburgh

CORONATION AND JUBILEES

It took a year after the death of King William IV, and the announcement that the young Princess Victoria was now the monarch, for the new queen's coronation to be prepared. On the morning of her coronation day, 28 June 1838, Victoria wrote in her journal:

I was awoke at four o'clock by the guns in the Park, and could not get much sleep afterwards on account of the noise of the people, bands, etc., etc. Got up at seven, feeling strong and well; the Park presented a curious spectacle, crowds of people up to Constitution Hill, soldiers, bands, etc. I dressed, having taken a little breakfast before I dressed, and a little after. At half-past 9 I went into the next room, dressed exactly in my House of Lords costume.

The press also recorded the day:

As early as three o'clock in the morning, the roar of artillery announced the arrival of the auspicious day on which the young Sovereign was to assume the crown of these realms.

    By six o'clock, the Mall, the Green Park, and the enclosure of St James's Park, were filled with persons of all ranks, and a regular struggle for places commenced. The police and military, however, soon afterwards arrived; and those who fancied they had secured the best places were speedily compelled to give way. Squadrons of the Life Guard, in their State dresses, gave animation and picturesqueness to the scene. The bands struck up God save the Queen! and the whole presented a scene of gaiety such as few ever behold.... On top of the triumphal arch at the Queen's Palace, some sailors were placed, to unfurl the Royal Standard of England, as the signal to mark the time of her Majesty quitting the Palace. As her Majesty entered her carriage, the tars, with three cheers, unfurled the "meteor flag" that for "a thousand years had braved the battle and the breeze". At this moment the sun, which had all the morning been clouded, shone forth in all its splendour; and the cheering of the tars was taken up by the countless thousands around, and continued until the Royal cortege had passed over Constitution Hill. Her Majesty seemed in excellent health and spirits, and bowed repeatedly in acknowledgment of her reception.

Carlisle Journal, Saturday, 7 July 1838

In 1887, Queen Victoria celebrated her Golden Jubilee (the date being counted from her accession to the throne, not her coronation) after 50 years as queen. In 1897, she celebrated her Diamond Jubilee, which commemorated 60 years as monarch. Both were spectacular occasions that boosted the British economy, especially in terms of tourism, as people travelled from all over the British Empire to witness the spectacle. They also made the royal family, and the Queen in particular, much more popular among the British people. Today, many towns and villages around Britain still maintain statues of Queen Victoria that date from one of the jubilee years. Throughout the 1870s, the Queen's popularity had been at an all-time low as she continued to mourn Prince Albert and shun royal duties, but by the mid-1880s, as her Golden Jubilee approached, she started to become more popular. By the time of her Diamond Jubilee, her reputation was fully restored and millions of people flocked to her jubilee procession and thronged the streets during her many jubilee visits.

The illustrator Ernest H. Shepherd wrote in his memoirs about the Queen's Diamond Jubilee parade in London:

> *The little old lady, a bonnet with a white osprey feather on her head, and a black-and-white parasol in her hand, kept bowing to left and right. She looked pale. We learnt afterwards that she was overcome more by the warmth of her reception south of the river than by the heat of the day. Indeed she nearly broke down, the tears streaming down her face. There could be no doubt what she meant to her people.*
> **From *Drawn from Life*, first published in 1957**

CHANGING TIMES

In 1897, an encyclopaedia was published by Love & Wyman to commemorate the Queen's Golden Jubilee. It reflected upon the past 60 years and how British society had changed during the Victorian years.

> *Moral and Political Ideas Sixty Years Ago*
> *In 1837, one discerns already the influence of new opinions and ideas in conflict with old ones. The new ideas which were, so to speak, in the air, had found expression in the poetry of Cowper, Wordsworth, Coleridge, Shelley, Byron, and Burns. The doctrine underlying these new phrases of thought was the Brotherhood of Man. All mankind were brothers,*

irrespective of race, creed or social rank; whence it followed that slavery, warfare, duelling, and all acts of violence were to be deprecated as crimes against humanity. No man should be allowed to tyrannise over his fellows; even criminals must be treated with some consideration, and punishment ought to be reformatory, not revengeful. Cruelty to animals was unsparingly condemned, and the most popular forms of sport were denounced as demoralising. Against such views, a sturdy English conservatism, – not confined to any particular party or sect – protested vigorously. Authority must be upheld, or Society would be disorganised – witness the French Revolution! – so that human brotherhood was an impracticable ideal. Besides, we must maintain the prestige of our own country; and war was sometimes necessary - witness our recent struggle with Napoleon! As for slavery, some races were fitted by nature to govern, and others to serve; and subject races would fare badly if left to themselves. Kindness to criminals would only encourage crime, and the abolition of duelling and manly sports would tend to make men cowardly and pusillanimous, and would inevitably cause the race to degenerate. So said the opponents of the new teaching. In 1837, slavery had not been abolished in all British possessions, but the slaves in our colonies had been freed four years before, and twenty millions of money had been voted as compensation to the quondam slave-owners..... The causes that led to the Chartism movement were then active, and the workman of that day was prone to be attracted by the arguments and promises of the agitator, who taught him that the country was being governed for the exclusive benefit of lazy landowners and greedy capitalists.... Only three years before Her Majesty's Accession – in 1834, when several strikes were organised – old and half-forgotten statutes had been revived, and the law strained against six agricultural labourers, who were transported for belonging to "illegal societies".

From *The Victorian Era. 1837–1897. An Encyclopaedia of the Arts, Manufactures, and Commerce of the United Kingdom*

2

TRANSPORT, ENGINEERING AND TECHNOLOGY

The Victorians witnessed the greatest era of technological change that Britain had ever experienced. Not only were major breakthroughs made in terms of engineering, transport and science, but these changes came about with astonishing rapidity. The Victorian age has become renowned as the age of invention.

TRAVEL IN THE VICTORIAN AGE

At the start of Queen Victoria's reign, the horse-drawn carriage was the standard mode of travel. By the middle of her reign, railways had started to spread not just across the country but all over the British Empire, and by the end of the nineteenth century the first motor cars had arrived on the streets of Britain. One of the most pivotal changes to Victorian methods of transport was the harnessing of steam power.

By the early Victorian years, the condition of Britain's roads was slowly starting to improve, thanks to the revenue earned by toll roads (also known as turnpikes), where the toll money went towards repairing the roads. Despite this, the roads were still dangerous, with potholes and ditches often causing accidents (not helped by the fact that most public stagecoaches were dangerously overloaded). One roadway peril the Victorians no longer had to face was highwaymen. The last recorded highway robbery had taken place in 1831 – and, strangely, by the end of the nineteenth century, this once feared and deadly criminal had become a romanticized figure.

⚑ **Toll Roads.** In 1750, the Turnpike Trust was set up and, as people began to accept they needed to pay a toll for using main roads, the conditions of the roads began to improve. This also led to a reduction in traffic accidents caused by ruts and holes on the road surface.

WATERWAYS

During the Industrial Revolution, Britain's rivers and canals began to be seen as an effective means of transport. A huge network of canals was built and horse-drawn barges became a common sight. Towpaths were built so that horses could be walked along the side of the canals, pulling the barges. It was estimated that a horse connected to a canal boat was able to pull a load 10 times heavier than it could when pulling a cart on the road. By the time Queen Victoria came to the throne, all of Britain's major towns were connected either by natural rivers or manmade canals. The golden age of the canals drew to a close towards the end of the nineteenth century: manufacturers no longer needed the canal system for transportation, because the railway system had become so wide-ranging and was so much faster.

Some years earlier, the artist John Constable (who had died in the year Queen Victoria came to the throne) had painted *Flatford Mill ("Scene on a Navigable River")* (1816). Constable, like many of the Romantic painters, had seen the Industrial Revolution as negative and frightening. His painting, which became very popular after his death, served to remind Victorians of the pastoral tranquility of Georgian England.

⚑ By 1850, the British canal network encompassed 4,000 miles (6,440 km).

⚑ In cold winters, Britain's canals would be kept clear for traffic by ice-breaking barges with specially reinforced hulls.

- In 1700, the journey from London to Manchester took an average of four days. By 1880, the journey, via railway, took just four hours.

- By 1851, Britain had 7,000 miles (11,250 km) of railway. Each of the individual railway companies had its own coat of arms.

- At the start of the nineteenth century, the port of London was the busiest working port in the world.

SCOTTISH SHIPBUILDING

In the mid-nineteenth century, Scotland led the world in shipbuilding. Its shipyards at Glasgow and Dumbarton made more than half of all British steamships. The Fairfield shipyard on the River Clyde was Scotland's biggest shipyard.

THE REGENT'S CANAL EXPLOSION

In the early hours of 2 October 1874, the sound of an enormous explosion in central London could be heard for miles around. A barge named *Tilbury* had been travelling along the Regent's Canal laden with an extraordinarily eclectic load: nuts, sugar, straw, coffee, six barrels of petroleum and several tonnes of gunpowder. While the barge was travelling underneath the Macclesfield Bridge in Regent's Park, there was a series of explosions and the barge burst into flames. Charles Baxton (the captain of the barge), his assistant and a "labouring boy" were all killed instantly; the bridge was destroyed and a nearby barge was so badly damaged that it sank. A large number of buildings within a mile's range of the bridge also suffered severe losses, with walls and ceilings collapsing, roofs being blown off and windows shattering. The canal, which connected Limehouse in East London with the Paddington Canal in the centre of the city, was closed for four days.

The coroner found that three people had been killed by the explosion – although newspaper reports also wrote of a person in a nearby house who had "died from fright". Several local residents were injured after having been hurled out of their beds by the force of the explosion or being hit by flying objects, and many thought they were experiencing an earthquake. Several shocked householders feared that their newly installed gas lighting might have caused the explosion.

One of those who witnessed the explosion was a barge labourer named William White. The *Tilbury* had been just one of a long string of barges, connected and being pulled together by one tug boat. Considering how many people were working on the string of barges (which were owned by the Grand Junction Canal Company), it was remarkable that so few were killed. At the coroner's inquest, William White reported:

> *We had come up from the City Basin. When we came up to the North Bridge I heard a small report on the* Tilbury*. I saw no lightning. There was a flash which seemed to light up the cabin. The steerer called out, "That's nearly blowed me out of the hatches already," Then I asked him "What was up?" I never remember his answering. The men shouted stop, and the boat behind the tug shouted also. The men on the* Tilbury *answered also. They had time to do that. The engine slackened its speed. There was time then to shout, "It's all right; go ahead, go steady." The engine went on a little way. Our boat was just leaving the bridge when the explosion occurred.... As soon as the* Tilbury *came up underneath the bridge I saw a flash. I remember no more. I lost my senses, feeling and everything. I am sure there were two reports. The first one was like the report of a small firearm.... When we heard the explosion we had no lamp burning. I never knew we carried gunpowder. We did not know at the time we were away that it was powder. We had no notice from anyone about the nature of the cargo. We act on the captain's instructions. I was never cautioned to be careful. I never smoke. Some of the boatmen smoke. I was never in the cabin of the* Tilbury.

Another person to give evidence at the inquest was a local resident, Dr Alfred Taylor, who also happened to be Professor of Chemistry at Guy's Hospital. Taylor said at the inquest, "I have seen the barges going along during the winter months, and the sparks shooting out of the tug like a luminous meteor." He recommended that no naked flames should be permitted on board the barges and that instead the workers should be given "Davy Lamps" (a safety lamp that had been invented in 1815).

STEAM ENGINES

The first steam engine in Britain was developed a decade and a half before Queen Victoria's birth by a Cornishman named Richard Trevithick, whose name is too often forgotten. Trevithick's work inspired the inventions of George Stephenson, who built the first working steam locomotive.

George Stephenson finished working on the *Rocket* in 1829. He was not the only engineer working with this exciting new technology, but his is the name remembered by history, because the *Rocket* beat all competitors at the pivotal Rainhill Trials. Spectators watched in awe when, on its final lap, the *Rocket* made – and maintained – a speed of 29 miles (47 km) per hour. It was the beginning of the Steam Age.

The first passenger railway line in Britain was the Stockton to Darlington line, which opened in 1825. By 1830, Stephenson's famed *Rocket* was working on the Manchester to Liverpool railway line, and in 1838, the first line between Birmingham and London had been built. By the middle of Queen Victoria's reign, steam trains and railways could be seen throughout Britain, but the journey towards modernizing Britain's transport system was not always an easy one. The railways cut through the British countryside, displacing communities and terrifying the general public. Stories abounded about terrible trains that caused illnesses in people and animals. Trains and the railways were credited with terrifying farm animals, spooking horses into bolting, or causing sheep and cows to miscarry and cows to stop producing milk.

The first shock of a great earthquake had, just at that period, rent the whole neighbourhood to its centre. Traces of its course were visible on every side. Houses were knocked down; streets broken through and stopped; deep pits and trenches dug in the ground; enormous heaps of earth and clay thrown up; buildings that were undermined and shaking, propped by great beams of wood. Here, a chaos of carts, overthrown and jumbled together, lay topsy-turvy at the bottom of a steep unnatural hill; there, confused treasures of iron soaked and rusted in something that had accidentally become a pond. Everywhere were bridges that led nowhere; thoroughfares that were wholly impassable; Babel towers of chimneys, wanting half their height; temporary wooden houses and enclosures, in the most unlikely situations; carcases of ragged tenements, and fragments of unfinished walls and arches, and piles of scaffolding, and wildernesses of bricks, and giant forms of cranes, and tripods straddling above nothing. There were a hundred thousand shapes and substances of incompleteness, wildly mingled out of their places, upside down, burrowing in the earth, aspiring in the air, mouldering in the water, and unintelligible as any dream. Hot springs and fiery eruptions, the usual attendants upon earthquakes, lent their contributions of confusion to the scene. Boiling water hissed and heaved within dilapidated walls; whence, also, the glare and roar of flames came issuing forth; and mounds of ashes blocked up rights of way, and wholly changed the law and custom of the neighbourhood.

In short, the yet unfinished and unopened Railroad was in progress; and, from the very core of all this dire disorder, trailed smoothly away, upon its mighty course of civilisation and improvement.

From *Dombey and Son* by Charles Dickens, 1848

By 1870, there were more than 100,000 steam engines on the railway tracks around Britain.

THE FIRST RAILWAY DEATH

The Right Honourable William Huskisson MP was the first person killed on the railways – a death which would have huge impact on decades ahead. . He died on 15 September 1830, the day on which the Liverpool to Manchester railway line was being opened. Huskisson was run over by the *Rocket*, which was steaming along at 24 miles per hour (39 kph). George Stephenson immediately drove him, on another locomotive called *Northumbrian*, to get medical help, but Huskisson died from his injuries.

Huskisson had been in a stationery train carriage parked on track alongside that which the *Rocket* was travelling on, having been invited to watch the ceremonial opening of the railway by the Duke of Wellington, whose cabinet he had resigned from a couple of years earlier. The two men appeared to have an angry discussion and Huskisson left. He stepped out of the wrong side of the carriage and onto the track directly in front of the *Rocket*.

QUEEN VICTORIA'S FIRST TRAIN JOURNEY

The Queen first travelled by train on 13 June 1842. She had been staying at Windsor Castle in order to take a train from nearby Slough station to London Paddington, on her way back to Buckingham Palace. She wrote in her journal: "The saloon we travelled in, on the train was very large & beautifully filled up. It took us exactly 30 minutes going to Paddington, & the motion was very slight, & much easier than a carriage, also no dust or great heat, — in fact, it was delightful, & so quick."

ROBERT STEPHENSON (1803–59)

Born to the railway engineer George Stephenson and his wife, Frances, Robert was three years old when his mother died. For a while, he was looked after by his uncle (after whom he had been named) and his aunt.

In 1815, he began working with his father and together they designed the "Geordie" safety lamp. Four years later, he became an apprentice mining engineer at Killingworth Colliery. He also worked with his father on the Stockton and Darlington Railway. In 1822, he worked as a surveyor on the Liverpool and Manchester Railway, but he left two years later to sail to South America and work in the silver-mine industry in Colombia. While he was away, his father set up George Stephenson and Son, with Robert Stephenson named as the company's chief engineer. The two men worked together on numerous projects, most famously on the *Rocket*.

After returning from Colombia and working in Newcastle and London, Robert Stephenson became one of the top names in the railway industry. He married Frances Sanderson and they moved to London, where Stephenson was appointed chief engineer on the London to Birmingham railway. In the 1840s, the passing of the Gauge Act made Robert Stephenson's newly patented railway gauge the standard size for British railways. This influence spread throughout the British Empire, making Stephenson – who had been born into an impoverished home – a very wealthy man. Sadly, his wife died young in 1842 and did not witness his greatest successes. In 1850, Queen Victoria offered Robert Stephenson a knighthood but he refused it. Despite this rebuff, he was appointed Royal Commissioner for the Great Exhibition of 1851.

Robert Stephenson built, or oversaw the building of, a large number of railway bridges. The most famous of his bridges in the UK is the Britannia Bridge in North Wales, which spans the Menai Strait. His many overseas projects included the Victoria Bridge in Montreal and several bridges over the Nile in Egypt. Robert Stephenson died four days before his fifty-sixth birthday. His fame was such that he was buried in Westminster Abbey.

ISAMBARD KINGDOM BRUNEL (1806–59)

The greatest engineer of the Victorian age, Brunel's works include the Clifton Suspension Bridge, the Great Western Railway, Paddington Station in London, and the steamships the SS *Great Western*, SS *Great Britain* and SS *Great Eastern*. From childhood, Brunel was absorbed in a world of engineering, as he was the only son of the celebrated French engineer Marc Brunel and his English wife Sophia Kingdom. As Isambard Brunel was born in Portsmouth and went to school in Brighton, he was surrounded by the shipping world, and it is unsurprising that he went on to become one of the most famous ship engineers in British history. He grew up bilingual in English and French, and at the age of 14 was sent to Caen and Paris to study mathematics.

While still a teenager, Brunel worked with his father on a truly remarkable project. The two men wanted to build a tunnel under the English Channel to connect England and France. In order to prove that such an underwater tunnel was possible, they began with a tunnel under the River Thames in East London, on which they started work in 1823. Despite the success of the Thames Tunnel, the Brunels' Channel tunnel was never commissioned since Queen Victoria and successive governments feared it would open up Britain to French invasion and war.

In 1828, a flood swept through the Thames Tunnel while Brunel was working on the site, and he was severely injured. He was sent to Bristol as a convalescent, and while there became aware of a competition to design a bridge over the Avon Gorge. In 1829, he drew up designs for the Clifton Suspension Bridge. Although his designs were eventually accepted (after a few modifications), he was never to see one of his most famous projects come to fruition, as a lack of funds meant that the bridge was not completed until 1864, five years after his death.

At the age of just 27, Brunel was invited to be the chief engineer on an ambitious new project, the Great Western Railway (GWR) between Bristol and London. He was a controversial chief, and at one point threatened to resign when he felt his plans were being held back, and in protest at the suggestion he should work with another engineer. However, his work paid off and the line became an icon of railway history. He was also commissioned to remodel London's Paddington Station; the Great Exhibition was being planned and the modest buildings at Paddington were deemed unsuitable for the anticipated huge crowds arriving in London to visit the exhibition. The station was intended to emulate Joseph Paxton's design for the Crystal Palace; Brunel's ideas were criticized by other architects as being too radical – but they worked.

Having harnessed the power of the railways, Brunel decided to look further afield, into the arena of trans-Atlantic travel. After helping to found the Great Steamship Company, he set about building a steamship that could make the journey from Bristol to New York in record time. The SS *Great Britain* was the first in a notable line of iron ships, and the largest ship in the world. She was also the first ocean-going ship to have a screw propeller and an iron hull. A leviathan in the shipping world, the SS *Great Britain* made the journey to New York in just 15 days.

In 1853, Brunel was commissioned to build the SS *Great Eastern*. His first ship, the SS *Great Western* (1837), had been a paddle steamer that travelled in the deep waters of the Atlantic Ocean (until she was overshadowed by her brilliant iron younger sister). The SS *Great Eastern* was to have a screw propeller, like the SS *Great Britain*, but this time it would have to operate in very different climatic conditions and in much shallower water in India. The project was fraught with difficulties and the SS *Great Eastern* was destined never to make it to India – and Brunel never to see her completed. On 5 September 1859, he was supervising the works when he collapsed with a heart attack on the ship's deck and died 10 days later. His funeral was attended not only by family and friends – including Robert Stephenson, with whom he had developed a good friendship – but also by hundreds of his engineering peers, whose profession had been changed forever by his work, and by thousands of railway workers.

⛄ During the course of his extraordinary career, Isambard Kingdom Brunel built more than 100 bridges, 25 railway lines, three of the world's most famous ships, eight docks and an army field hospital that was used in the Crimean War (it was prefabricated for easy transportation).

The Times wrote a glowing obituary of Isambard Kingdom Brunel. It included the words:

> *While noticing these great efforts to improve the art of shipbuilding, it must not be forgotten that Mr Brunel, we believe, was the first man of eminence in his profession who perceived the capabilities of the screw as a propeller. He was brave enough to stake a great reputation upon the soundness*

*of the reasoning upon which he had based his conclusions....
It would hardly be just ... to conclude this notice without
allusion to his private character and worth. Few men were
more free from that bane of professional life – professional
jealousy. He was always ready to assist others, and to do
justice to their merits.*

The Times, **September 1859**

RAILWAY DISASTERS

Rednal, 7 June 1865

Thirteen people died and around 30 people were injured due to
the derailment of a passenger train, travelling at high speed, on
the Shrewsbury to Chester railway line. The accident happened as the train
was approaching Rednal station in Shropshire. The driver was unable
to stop the speeding train in time, after seeing the flags put up by the
railway maintenance workers who were working on the line; part of the
blame was placed on the engineering of the train which was deemed not
to have good enough brakes.

Staplehurst, 9 June 1865

In the nineteenth century, the boat train from France travelled via Kent
to London, adhering to a tidal timetable. On 9 June 1865, a group of
railway workers downed tools while working on the track of a railway
bridge over the River Beult, erroneously believing that day's train had
already gone past. At around 3pm, as the train neared Staplehurst in
Kent, it hit the loosened railway plates on the bridge. Eight first-class
carriages at the front of the train lurched off the bridge and into the
water below. There were more than 100 passengers on the train. Ten
people were killed and 14 more were seriously injured.

Two of the passengers on the train, whose carriage had come to a stop
just before hitting the water, were the novelist Charles Dickens and his
secret mistress, the actress Ellen Ternan. Dickens was one of the survivors
who helped pull others from the wreckage. A popular story of the day,
which was shown in the illustrated papers, was of the world-famous
author filling his top hat with water to take to the injured.

Dickens wrote to his friend Frederic Ouvry that the accident had been "under-stated in the papers this morning". To another friend, the banking heiress Angela Burdett-Coutts, he wrote, in shaky handwriting very unlike his usual firm hand: "I was in the carriage that did not go over the bridge but caught in turning and hung suspended over the ruined brick work.... I could not have imagined so appalling a scene."

Abergele, 20 August 1868

Thirty-three people were killed, and many more injured, following a collision between two trains near the Welsh town of Abergele. Six days later, *The Blackburn Standard* reported:

> *One of those frightful railways accidents, which happen too frequently, occurred on Thursday at noon, at Abergele between Chester and Holyhead. From information which we have received, it would seem that the Irish limited mail train, which left Chester at 11.47 on Thursday forenoon for Holyhead, shortly after leaving Abergele, came into collision whilst coming round a curve in the line with a number of waggons [sic] which, owing to the severance of the coupling-chains, had become detached from a luggage train preceding the mail train.... The effect of the collision was frightful. The waggons severed from the luggage train were laden with a large quantity of petroleum oil, and upon the engine coming into collision with them, the oil was set on fire.*
>
> *The Blackburn Standard*, 26 August 1868

> *Fly by steam-force the country across,*
> *Faster than jockey outside a race-horse:*
> *With time-bills mismanaged, fast trains after slow,*
> *You shall have danger wherever you go.*
> "Ride a Cock-Horse" (a parody), from *Punch*, 9 October 1852

BOOKS AND THE RAILWAY

In 1848, an enterprising bookseller opened a stall at Euston station in London. His name was William Henry Smith and he ran a business with his son (of the same name), by the name of W.H. Smith & Son. The entrepreneur recognized early what a phenomenon the new "railway craze" would become and began investing in special books for the new breed of traveller. The books were small, slim and inexpensive paperbacks known as "yellowbacks", because of their distinctive mustard-yellow covers. Shortly after the first W.H. Smith railway stall was opened, the publisher George Routledge began producing a series of inexpensive novels also aimed at the train traveller, known as the Railway Library.

In 1878, a railway worker named Alexander Anderson published a volume of verses entitled *Songs of the Rail*. He dedicated it to "My Fellow-Workers on the Railway". In his preface to the book, he wrote the following:

> *Some critics, in "reviewing" a former work of mine, took exception to the railway poems it contained as being exaggerated in incident and over-drawn in treatment. In reply to these criticisms, I beg to remark that nearly all my railway poems are founded upon facts, and not a few of them upon incidents that have taken place upon a line on which I work.... I send out this volume, like former ones, in the hope that it may interest my fellow-workers on the railway ... however humble may be their position. I trust that its perusal may lead the engine-driver, among others, to look upon his "iron horse" as the embodiment of a force as noble as gigantic ... a power destined, beyond doubt, to be one of the civilisers of the world.*

> *"Shall we go and sit in the cathedral?" he asked, when their meal was finished.*
> *"Cathedral? Yes. Though I think I'd rather sit in the*

railway station," she answered, a remnant of vexation still in her voice. "That's the centre of the town life now. The cathedral has had its day!"

From *Jude the Obscure* by Thomas Hardy, 1895

THE GREAT WESTERN RAILWAY

The GWR was founded on 31 May 1835. The headquarters were at Paddington in central London and the railway line ran to the southwest, to Bristol and eventually to Cornwall. The first superintendent of the GWR was in charge of 707 men.

The first Regulation of Railways Act was passed in 1840. It introduced safety inspections and gave a list of offences including "impeding or obstructing engines", and prohibited railway staff from drinking or being drunk on duty.

PENNY FARTHINGS

Invented in the early 1870s by James Starley, the penny farthing was one of the first styles of bicycle to be seen on the streets of Britain and was popular until the 1890s. The design was named after the penny and farthing coins, as the front wheel was so much bigger (penny) than the back wheel (farthing). However, the nickname by which it is most commonly known was not its original name – at the start of its career the penny-farthing was known as the "high wheeler".

MOTOR CARS

When the first cars made their way to Britain, motoring enthusiasts were infuriated by the limitations imposed on them. In the early 1890s, it was a legal requirement that any "self-propelled vehicle" was forbidden to travel on public roads at any speed higher than 4 mph (6.5 kph); cars also needed to be preceded by a man walking in front of them waving a red warning flag. The act was repealed in 1896.

THOMAS CRAPPER (1836–1910)

Born in a Yorkshire town to a working-class family, Thomas Crapper was apprenticed at the age of 14 to a London plumber and quickly showed aptitude for his profession. In 1861, he set up his own plumbing company, Thomas Crapper & Co., in London's Chelsea. In addition to his plumbing work, he was also an inspired inventor who registered nine patents. He has become famous as the inventor of the flushing lavatory – although this isn't actually correct. The first flushing loo was in existence as long ago as the reign of Elizabeth I. What Crapper invented was a flushing lavatory that worked consistently, largely thanks to a ballcock system for refilling the cistern after the flush.

One of Crapper's innovative ideas was to set up the very first "bathroom showroom" in Britain, showcasing bathroom fittings in his large shop window in London. The sight of bathrooms fixtures – including even the most intimate of bathroom accessories – on full view was claimed to be so shocking that it caused society ladies to faint.

CRAPPER FACTS

- Contrary to popular belief, Thomas Crapper's surname did not give rise to the slang word "crap"; the word had been in existence for several centuries before Crapper invented the flushing loo and probably derives from Medieval Latin.
- Every patent that Thomas Crapper registered was accepted.
- By the 1880s, Thomas Crapper & Co. Ltd were able to advertise themselves as Sanitary Engineers to the royal household, having been commissioned to work for the Prince of Wales (the future King Edward VII). Over the next few years, Crapper products could be seen at Sandringham, Windsor Castle and Buckingham Palace.

3

THE VICTORIAN HOME

Throughout the nineteenth century, the ideal of the Victorian home changed greatly. In the past, there had been huge estates owned by the country's wealthiest people while most of the population lived either in slums or in small residences on land owned by the gentry (which were rented out). In Victorian Britain, many wealthy families found themselves needing to sell off their land. As the wealth had slowly started to shift from the upper to the middle classes, more people were now in a position to build or buy instead of renting.

As increasing numbers of people moved from the country to cities, far more urban homes had to be created and neighbourhoods began to change; it was not unusual to find new developments of expensive homes being built alongside terrible slums. As the middle classes grew exponentially – due to the new wealth created by the Industrial Revolution, as well as to opportunities for making money becoming available in far-flung parts of the British Empire – many more middle-class residences were needed. It was also the beginning of suburbia, with improved public transport allowing people to live in one place and work in another.

AT THE ROYAL TABLE

An average dinner in the royal household consisted of between four and six courses, with anything from seven to nine dishes in each course. At the start of Queen Victoria's reign, it was usual for all the food to be placed upon the table, and for the guests to help themselves or be helped by servants. This changed in the mid-Victorian era, when the fashion for service *à la Russe* ("in the Russian style") came into mode. Fashionable in Paris from the early 1800s, the style was for servants to bring in the dishes for each course and to serve people individually. This suited chefs much better, as their food could be served fresh and hot. It did not, however, always suit guests at the royal table.

Queen Victoria was notorious for the rapidity with which she could eat. She was always served first and would start eating immediately, while the lowliest or youngest guests who were seated furthest away from the Queen would be served last. As everyone at the table had to stop eating as soon as the Queen had finished, her children and less important invited guests often complained that they had been unable to eat anything – the servers would not have had time to reach them by the time the monarch had wolfed down her food and the plates were being cleared to prepare for the next course.

⤨ For the Queen's Diamond Jubilee banquet, 24 chefs were brought over to London from Paris to help prepare the feast.

> *The street-trade in ginger-beer – now a very considerable traffic – was not known to any extent until about thirty years ago. About five years ago "fountains" for the production of ginger-beer became common in the streets. The largest and handsomest ginger-beer fountain in London was – I speak of last summer – in use at the East-end, usually standing in Petticoat-lane, and is the property of a dancing master.*
>
> From **London Labour and the London Poor**
> by Henry Mayhew, 1851

PRESERVING FOOD

For centuries, cooks, farmers, food manufacturers and entrepreneurs had been experimenting with different ways of keeping food fresh. Since the 1810s, food had been sold in iron cans lined with tin, but it often spoilt despite this attempt to preserve it and no one was sure why. Then, in

1857, the French chemist Louis Pasteur discovered that one of the chief reasons for food spoiling was the presence of bacteria. This led to new ways of preserving foods, including the pasteurization that bore his name and was most famous for eliminating diseases in milk. The discovery spawned a prosperous new industry in tinned foods. By the 1870s, tinned food was on the increase and meant that food could be kept much longer.

Early experiments with freezing food had seldom been successful, but in the 1870s a new method of refrigerating food was being tried. There was great excitement in 1880 when a cargo of still-frozen and still-edible meat arrived from Australia on board the cargo ship SS *Strathleven*. This led to a huge trend in importing food from overseas – and caused the profits of British farmers to start falling.

GOLDEN SYRUP

Lyle's Golden Syrup was one of the most iconic of new British food products in the nineteenth century. Abram Lyle, an entrepreneur and businessman, had built a sugar refinery on the banks of the River Thames and he wanted to make use of the golden-coloured liquid – which he called "Goldie" – that was a by-product of refining his cane sugar. Initially he started selling it in simple wooden cases from his factory. The arrival of really good food tins enabled him to start selling it in gold and green tins like those still characteristic today.

The tin was decorated with one of the strangest of branding logos: a dead lion with bees buzzing around its carcass, accompanied by the motto, "Out of the strong came forth sweetness". It was inspired by verses from the Old Testament.

CHOCOLATE

In 1853, the previously high rate of tax on imported cocoa beans was relaxed, and the British love affair with chocolate began in earnest. Chocolate was initially known only in the form of drinking cocoa, an exotic and expensive drink that had been popular in the coffee houses of eighteenth-century Britain. Drinking chocolate was also given a boost by the growing Temperance movement, which advocated teetotalism. One of the most popular Temperance drinks was drinking chocolate, which was claimed to be as stimulating as alcohol without being intoxicating.

TEA

Throughout the Victorian age, people in every social class drank tea. In earlier decades, tea had been considered medicinal; later it became fashionable but very expensive and the preserve of the upper classes. By the 1860s, however, a report claimed that 99 per cent of the poorest working-class families were now tea drinkers. In the earliest years of Queen Victoria's reign, Chinese green tea was still the most widely imported, but by the end of the nineteenth century it was too expensive for most pockets. The newest drink was black tea, usually from Indian or Ceylon (present day Sri Lanka), which was much cheaper.

A RECIPE FOR ICED-PUDDING

In her *Book of Household Management*, Mrs Beeton included information about how to make several types of iced desserts, including the following "Parisian" recipe:

INGREDIENTS.—$^1/_2$ lb. of sweet almonds, 2 oz. of bitter ones, $^3/_4$ lb. of sugar, 8 eggs, $1^1/_2$ pints of milk.
Mode.—Blanch and dry the almonds thoroughly in a cloth, then pound them in a mortar until reduced to a smooth paste; add to these the well-beaten eggs, the sugar, and milk; stir these ingredients over the fire until they thicken, but do not allow them to boil; then strain and put the mixture into the freezing-pot; surround it with ice, and freeze it as directed in recipe 1290. When quite frozen, fill an iced-pudding mould, put on the lid, and keep the pudding in ice until required for table; then turn it out on the dish, and garnish it with a compôte of any fruit that may be preferred, pouring a little over the top of the pudding. This pudding may be flavoured with vanilla, Curaçao, or Maraschino.
Time.—$^1/_2$ hour to freeze the mixture.
Seasonable.—Served all the year round.

At the start of Queen Victoria's reign, tea rooms and cafes started to be seen as an alternative to pubs, and the Temperance movement was quick to capitalize on their popularity. By the late Victorian age, they had become a largely female domain, a safe haven for women to meet each other or simply to take tea by themselves, without being censured for not being chaperoned.

ICE CREAM

Ice cream had grown in popularity throughout Europe since the seventeenth century, and in 1718 a recipe book published in London, *Mrs Mary Eales's Receipts*, had included a recipe for ice cream. By the time of Queen Victoria's reign, ice cream was widely available to all the social classes and the Queen mentions "ices" frequently in her journal. At the end of 1839, two years after becoming queen, she recorded in her journal a conversation with Lord Melbourne about the need for a royal ice cellar, "[he] quite agreed, and said, he would see what could be done ... about building an ice cellar, as the expense of getting ice was so enormous".

THE PENNY LICK

While the wealthy built ice houses to feed their addiction to ice cream, the poorest people could buy what was known as a "penny lick". These were sold by street vendors on thick glass bowls, which were mostly solid glass with just a small dimple in the top into which a small portion of ice cream could be placed. Customers could buy a halfpenny lick, a penny lick or a tuppenny [two pence] lick. The glass bowl was owned by the ice cream vendor and was used for everyone who came to the stall – the rules of catering hygiene were still in their infancy. Following an outbreak of cholera in the 1870s, one of the several culprits blamed for the spread of the disease was the filthy penny lick glasses. In 1899, penny licks were banned by law in London, as they were believed to be responsible for the spread of consumption (the name given to tuberculosis).

⧉ For part of Queen Victoria's reign, there was a heavy tax imposed on sugar. When it was withdrawn in 1874, sweets and sweet things became very fashionable.

Children's food should be nourishing rather than stimulating. They do not need much meat, nor require several courses to make a meal. The meals should be served regularly at the same hour daily, and irregular eating of sweets, cake, biscuits, fruit etc., between meals should not be permitted…. The most important thing is to vary the food given; for children, like ourselves, need change of diet. A good dinner from a joint one day may be followed the next by one of macaroni boiled in milk. When the children are young, soup or fish makes a pleasant change; while puddings should be not only more frequent, but more varied in flavour than those usually given to children…. Plenty of milk should be given to young children, for it is their best and most natural food.

From *The Book of Household Management* by Mrs Isabella Beeton, 1861

COOKERY WRITERS

Mrs Beeton is the most famous Victorian author on household management, but she was not the first. In 1845, two famous cookery books were published: celebrity chef Charles Francatelli published his bestseller *The Modern Cook*, and Eliza Acton published *Modern Cookery for Private Families*. Acton's work was also a bestseller, until it was eclipsed by that of Mrs Beeton. In 1846, Alexis Soyer, the chef at London's prestigious Reform Club, published *The Gastronomic Regenerator*, which was reputed to have sold around 60,000 copies within a fortnight.

A RECIPE FOR MADELEINES

These are made with the same kind of batter as Genoese cakes, to which currants, dried cherries, candied peel or angelica may be added. When the batter is ready, let it be poured into a sufficient number of small fluted or plain dariole or madeleine moulds (previously buttered inside); these must be placed on a baking-sheet spread with some charcoal ashes, to the depth of half an inch, and then baked in an oven of a moderate heat. When they are done, turn them out of the moulds, and dish them up in a pyramid form. These cakes may also be partially emptied, then filled up with some kind of preserve, and the small circular piece, removed previously to taking out the crumb, should be replaced.

From *The Modern Cook* by Charles Elme Francatelli, 1845

ELIZA ACTON (1799–1859)

A poet as well as a cook, Eliza Acton studded her book, *Modern Cookery for Private Families*, with witty references. One of her recipes is for "Publisher's Pudding", filled with expensive ingredients – it is in contrast to a simple recipe of cheap ingredients entitled "The Poor Author's Pudding". She was the first British cookery author to put ingredients into a separate section for ease of reference – until this time, recipes were a piece of literary prose and cooks had to read all the way through to work out what ingredients they needed. Sadly, over the years Eliza Acton has been forgotten and Mrs Beeton is usually credited with having introduced this new way of writing recipes. Although Acton became famed for her family recipes, she was a single woman with no children who lived with her mother and one servant.

In 1851 a new cookery book entitled *What Shall We Have for Dinner?* was published under the pseudonym of Lady Maria Clutterbuck; in reality the author was Catherine Dickens, wife of the novelist Charles Dickens. The book included recipes inspired by Catherine's Scottish ancestry and childhood, as well as several Dickens family favourites and dishes discovered during her foreign travels. She also credited a few famous chefs whose recipes she included. *What Shall We Have for Dinner?* was advertised as a guide for young wives and promised to offer "bills of fare" for between two and 18 people.

The book is practical and assumes that the cook will almost certainly be a woman working in a limited kitchen; it includes simple and more complicated recipes, as well as many that make use of the most inexpensive ingredients for those families on a limited budget. The menus are divided into months, to take advantage of the ingredients that would be available in each season. A recipe that appears again and again within the suggested menus is "Toasted Cheese", which just happened to be one of Charles Dickens's favourite savouries (a savoury was a popular final course in Victorian Britain, served after the sweet pudding course).

A RECIPE FOR POTATO BALLS

Bake the potatoes, mash them very nicely, make them into balls, rub them over with the yolk of an egg, and put them into the oven or before the fire to brown. These balls may be varied by the introduction of a third portion of grated ham or tongue.

From *What Shall We Have For Dinner?* by Catherine Dickens, 1851

CHARLES ELME FRANCATELLI (1805–67)

Born in London to an Italian father and a British mother, Francatelli moved to Paris as a teenager to study cookery. On returning to England, he cooked for some of the country's wealthiest people, but was horrified to see how much food was thrown away while the poor were starving. He famously claimed that he would be able to cater for most of London's starving families just by using leftovers from the tables of the rich.

In 1854, Francatelli took over from Alexis Soyer at the Reform Club in London and his celebrity was assured. Following the success of his book *The Modern Cook*, he decided to write for a new market and *A Plain Cookery Book for the Working Classes* was published in 1852. In 1861, he published *The Cook's Guide and Housekeeper & Butler's Assistant*, which had the subtitle "A Practical Treatise on English and Foreign Cookery in all its Branches". Francatelli shared his love of sweet recipes in *Royal English and Foreign Confectionary Book*, published in 1862. He died in Eastbourne, having retired just a few months previously.

VICTORIAN KITCHENS

At the start of Queen Victoria's reign, very few houses had their own water supply, particularly in the countryside. Most people had to transport water from their local well, or pay someone else to deliver water for them. In towns, there was always a water carrier, although those who could not afford to pay for his services went to the public fountains or pumps to collect water. Many of the public water sources were contaminated with waterborne diseases.

Ice was also a much-sought-after commodity, both for keeping foods cool and for making essential items such as ice cream. In addition to a water carrier, most towns also had an ice man, who would supply blocks of ice to cooks and households. Bigger houses with gardens often had their own ice house – this was dug underground to ensure it stayed cool. During the winter, ice and snow would be packed into it in the hope that it would remain cool throughout the summer months.

The poorest homes did not possess ovens. If people living in slums and poor housing wanted hot food, it needed either to be cooked on a fire or taken to the local bakery. Bakers charged people to heat up food in their ovens. These ovens could only be used when the bakeries were open but no longer needed to bake bread, which meant that there were very few times when working-class families could enjoy a hot meal. Because of religious laws, bakeries and other shops were not open on Sunday – in 1843, when he wrote *A Christmas Carol*, Charles Dickens used the character of Ebenezer Scrooge to voice his own anger over the situation:

> *In time the bells ceased, and the bakers were shut up; and yet there was a genial shadowing forth of all these dinners and the progress of their cooking, in the thawed blotch of wet above each baker's oven; where the pavement smoked as if its stones were cooking too.*
>
> *"Is there a peculiar flavour in what you sprinkle from your torch?" asked Scrooge.*
>
> *"There is. My own."*
>
> *"Would it apply to any kind of dinner on this day?" asked Scrooge.*
>
> *"To any kindly given. To a poor one most."*

> *"Why to a poor one most?" asked Scrooge.*
>
> *"Because it needs it most."*
>
> *"Spirit," said Scrooge, after a moment's thought, "I wonder you, of all the beings in the many worlds about us, should desire to cramp these people's opportunities of innocent enjoyment."*
>
> *"I!" cried the Spirit.*
>
> *"You would deprive them of their means of dining every seventh day, often the only day on which they can be said to dine at all," said Scrooge. "Wouldn't you?"*
>
> *"I!" cried the Spirit.*
>
> *"You seek to close these places on the Seventh Day," said Scrooge. "And it comes to the same thing!"*
>
> *"I seek!" exclaimed the Spirit.*
>
> *"Forgive me if I am wrong. It has been done in your name, or at least in that of your family," said Scrooge.*
>
> *"There are some upon this earth of yours", returned the Spirit, "who lay claim to know us, and who do their deeds of passion, pride, ill-will, hatred, envy, bigotry, and selfishness in our name, who are as strange to us and all our kith and kin, as if they had never lived. Remember that, and charge their doings on themselves, not us."*

Wealthier homes usually possessed an iron stove known as a "kitchen range". This was the bane of many Victorian servants' lives, as the ranges required so much cleaning, stoking and looking after. Most kitchen ranges ran on coal, which needed to be kept constantly topped up and produced a great deal of dirt. The range would need to be cleaned every day, which was usually the job of the lowliest kitchen maid. Her job would include getting up before the rest of the household to clean out the range (it was impossible to do this the night before as it would still be too hot). She would then stock up the coal and light the fires so that the range would be working for when the cook came down, and prepare hot water for the family's bathing and start cooking breakfast. The range's flue became sooty and blocked very quickly, and needed to be cleaned out regularly (usually once a week).

⚡ At the start of the nineteenth century, Britain had been producing fewer than 20 million tonnes of coal per year; by the year of Queen Victoria's death, coal production had risen to over 220 million tonnes per year.

By the 1880s, kitchen ranges were starting to become outdated and gas cookers had become popular. The first gas-fired ranges to be shown in Britain were at the Great Exhibition of 1851, but initially people were reluctant to trust gas, having heard stories of gas poisoning and gas explosions. Entrepreneurial companies started hiring out gas cookers so people could try them out first, and by the 1880s and 1890s, the most fashionable new homes were being equipped with gas cooking appliances.

In houses with kitchens, there would almost always be a separate scullery, even if it was only the size of a cupboard. The kitchen was for cooking, while the scullery was usually where the sink was kept and where all the messy food-preparation jobs were carried out. This kept poultry feathers, onion skins, potato peelings and other kitchen detritus out of the cook's way.

⚡ It was not uncommon for kitchens to have a resident pet: cats were kept to keep down mice and rats, and hedgehogs were kept to get rid of beetles and other insects.

MRS BEETON AND HOUSEHOLD MANAGEMENT

In 1861, Mrs Isabella Beeton published a book that changed British family life. *Mrs Beeton's Book of Household Management* was seen as an indispensable guide to every aspect of home care and cooking. Alongside recipes and cookery instructions, the author advised on buying and preserving food, how to store household items, the best cleaning methods for all types of products and materials, how to mend clothes, how to pack a picnic, how to plan a dinner party or a grand ball, and what the duties of servants should be.

SERVANTS

Many servants began work as children and worked very long hours. To be considered part of the middle classes, a person needed to have at least one servant. For those families struggling to feed themselves, let alone feed and pay the wages of a servant as well, the requisite servant often came to them from an orphanage or workhouse. They would usually be given bed and board alone, their "payment" coming from being "trained up". These children would be taught all the rudiments of cleaning, housekeeping and every other task necessary to find work as a domestic servants. The intention was that once they had been trained, they would be able to find paid work elsewhere.

Male servants could progress up the career ranks more easily than female servants, for whom there were far fewer opportunities of escaping the everyday drudgery. The most important job for a female servant was that of housekeeper. For a male servant, the most important job was that of butler. Both the butler and housekeeper would expect to have their own living quarters, and their own parlour or sitting room. Amongst the lowliest jobs were those of the scullery maid – who did all the most menial kitchen tasks, such as scrubbing vegetables, washing up and preparing the cook's ingredients – and the maid-of-all-work, who could be called upon at all hours of the day or night to carry out tasks. If any member of the household was still awake late into the night, a servant would need to be awake and working, even if they were required to be up again very early in the morning. Ironically, the most poorly paid servants usually worked much longer hours than anyone else in the household.

One of the great advantages of being a servant in a big house was being well fed. Unlike most working-class people, for whom food could be scarce and often of very poor quality, servants knew they would receive three good meals a day.

GOVERNESSES

Perhaps the most isolated servant in any family was the nursery governess, whose job was to teach the children. The governess lived in a strange middle world – she was not a below-stairs servant but neither was she of the same status as the family. Victorian literature held a special place in its romantic canon for governesses; they were seen as lonely figures of intelligent womanhood who were caught between the household's upstairs and downstairs worlds, existing somewhere in between.

The life of a governess was not always financially rewarding. Although she was employed, a governess was not considered a servant – which often meant her employer did not pay for her clothes or medical bills, nor take responsibility for her welfare. So many governesses found themselves in financial difficulty after losing a position or becoming ill that, in 1843, the Governesses' Benevolent Institution was set up. Its purpose was "for affording temporary assistance to governesses in distress; granting annuities to aged governesses; and to afford a home for governesses during the intervals between their engagements, on their paying a small sum weekly for board and lodging". It also provided "an asylum for aged governesses in connection with the above" – in this instance the word "asylum" was used to mean a refuge, not a psychiatric institution.

A GOOD GENERAL SERVANT WANTED. Must understand plain cooking and be clean. Teetotaller preferred. Nursemaid kept. Wages £18 to commence, which would be quickly increased to a really capable and reliable girl.

Advertisement from the *Daily Telegraph*, 1895

THE SERVANT PROBLEM

As more work opportunities opened up towards the end of the Victorian era, it was becoming increasingly difficult for people on a limited income to find – and retain – good servants. People who would previously have had no option but to go into domestic service could now get jobs in shops, banks, cafes, factories, pubs and in other businesses that had boomed after the Industrial Revolution and the rapid growth of the middle classes. One of the most hotly debated topics in middle-class drawings rooms became known as "the servant problem".

> *It is the duty of your servants to serve you honestly, vigilantly, and with exactness; but it is no less your duty to take care that they do so.*
>
> **From *The Philosophy of Help*, 1853**

Employers of servants spent much of their time worrying about their servants' morals, convinced that each of them was out to thieve and that most working-class women and girls were far more likely to be tempted into "sinning" than their own middle-class daughters. They worried that female servants would have male admirers or "followers", and many actually stipulated in adverts "no followers allowed". In the mid-Victorian era, rumours abounded of nursery maids and governesses drugging their charges with sleeping draughts and spending their days pleasing themselves instead of caring for the children (in reality, most were horribly overworked and often very lonely, having to sleep either in or alongside the children's nursery and enjoying little adult conversation). Employers kept their possessions locked away, more for fear of servants reading private letters or drinking their wine than for fear of burglars breaking in.

VICTORIAN CLEANING TIPS

- Stale bread was a popular cleaning product, as it could be used to soak up spills or to rub out older stains.
- To help keep ants out of the home, servants were advised to find out where they were coming from and then place strips of cucumber next to the entry points (ants were reputed to have an aversion to cucumber).
- Natural air fresheners could be made from citrus peel, cut into strands and hung by open windows.
- A method for getting rid of flies suggests:
  1) Place leeks in water and leave them for a day and night.
  2) Strain the liquid and bottle it.
  3) Dab it onto the furniture.
- Keeping an open dish of baking soda in the larder was recommended to absorb any unpleasant food smells.
- Many Victorian pans and cooking utensils were made from copper. To clean them, maids were recommended to rub the copper with

fresh sorrel leaves, or to wash the pans in a solution of water infused with sorrel leaves.

- Washing up cloths were disinfected by being boiled in water and vinegar.
- Windows were cleaned by mixing vinegar and water, and applying it to the glass with old newspaper. More newspaper was used to dry and polish the window panes.
- Lemon juice was used for multiple cleaning tasks, such as cleaning and whitening marble, ceramic and tiled surfaces. It was also used for cleaning stubborn dishes, which were left to soak in water with lemon juice added to it.
- Used tea leaves were carefully collected and used to clean carpets. The almost-dry tea leaves were sprinkled over carpets – dust and grit would cling to the tea leaves and then when the leaves were brushed away, the dirt would go with them. On sunny days, carpets would be hung outside on a line and beaten with a cane carpet beater to get rid of dust, grime and any insects that might be living in them. In winter, servants would hope for snow, as carpets could be taken outside and rolled in the snow, then dragged around leaving the dirt behind.

POISONS IN THE HOME

- To get rid of bed bugs, Victorians were advised to make a paste of egg whites and mercury, and brush it on to the mattress.
- Chloride of lime was poured into drains to unblock them. It was also used to disinfect bed sheets in sickrooms.
- Lye caustic soda dissolved in water was used to clean wooden floors. Many maids suffered bleach burns or poisoning from using it.
- One of the dangers lurking in every home was carbolic acid, which was a popular cleaning aid but also extremely poisonous. The newspapers were kept busy reporting deaths by carbolic poisoning – many of these were suicides, some were ill-concealed domestic murders and some were tragic accidents. It was noted that carbolic acid was often sold in packaging similar to that in which food products, such as baking soda, were sold, and that liquid carbolic acid was sold in similarly shaped bottles to beer.
- Arsenic was used in wallpapers, clothes dyes and in toiletries, such as Dr Mackenzie's Arsenical Soap.

ADVERT FOR CARBOLIC OINTMENT (1898)
CALVERT'S CARBOLIC OINTMENT
Is unequalled as a Remedy
for Piles, Throat Colds, Chapped Hands, Chilblains, Scalds,
Burns, Cuts, Earache, Neuralgic and Rheumatic Pains,
Ringworm, and Skin Ailments generally.

ADVERT FOR ARSENIC SOAP (1897)
SPECIALLY PREPARED AS A BEAUTIFIER OF THE SKIN
& COMPLEXION
Dr. Mackenzie's celebrated Arsenical Toilet Soap and
Complexion Wafers
Will produce the most lovely Complexion, free from blotch,
blemish, coarseness, redness, freckles, or pimples. Deliciously
and expensively perfumed. One shilling per Tablet. Doctor's
certificate with each cake, certifying to its harmlessness, purity,
and beautifying qualities. Beware of injurious imitations.

NEWSPAPER REPORTS OF CARBOLIC POISONING

On Wednesday afternoon a son of Mr John Johnston, formerly
a butler in Oxford, who came to reside in Montgomery Street,
on Saturday last, was fatally poisoned by drinking a quantity of
carbolic acid, which he had found in an attic. The child was only
two years old.

Dundee Courier, Friday, 3 July 1896

Another death from carbolic acid poisoning occurred in
Liverpool yesterday. The police were called to the house of a
man named Mealey, who said his wife had taken carbolic acid.
The woman, who was in a state of collapse, was removed to the
hospital, where, in spite of every attention, she died in a short

time. No fewer than 13 cases of poisoning by carbolic acid,
accidentally or premeditated, have occurred in Liverpool during
the month, five being fatal.

Manchester Courier, Saturday, 1 September 1888

Maggie Weir, a domestic servant, employed at 1 Broughton
Place, Edinburgh, was discovered in an unconscious condition
in the house last night, supposed to be suffering from the effects
of carbolic acid poisoning. She was taken to the Edinburgh
Royal Infirmary, where she lies in a serious condition. It is not at
present known how she came to take the liquid.

Edinburgh Evening News, Wednesday, 14 October 1896

At the start of Queen Victoria's reign, most British homes were lit by candles and oil lamps. By the end of the Queen's life, gas lighting had become commonplace and electricity was starting to be introduced.

4

THE ARTS

The Victorian Age saw huge changes in the arts world, and these, in turn, reflected the transformations taking place in society. Until the mid-Victorian age, conventionality ruled the day, but from the 1870s onwards, Britain began to witness sweeping changes. Increasing numbers of women were being recognized and accepted in the artistic professions, and the strictures that had been imposed upon the early Victorians began to be rebelled against. By the 1890s – a decade known as "the naughty nineties" – fine art, literature and the theatre had become much more liberal.

VICTORIAN LITERATURE

By the time Victoria ascended to the throne, the age of Romantic literature was in full sway, with sensationalist and gothic novels hugely popular as well as the poetry of John Keats, Percy Bysshe Shelley, Lord Byron and William Wordsworth (whom Victoria would make Poet Laureate in 1843).

Although the Queen herself disapproved heartily of novel reading (sacking her daughters' French governess after discovering she had permitted the princesses to read novels), the fashion for fiction thrived throughout the nineteenth century. Popular novelists, including Charles Dickens, Elizabeth Gaskell, George Eliot, Anthony Trollope, Wilkie Collins and William Thackeray, wrote their novels in instalments, which were serialized every week or month in popular magazines. As books were extremely expensive and magazines much more affordable, this method of serializing books meant that more people than ever before could afford to read novels.

Although the popular novels of the Victorian era are considered by today's schoolchildren as difficult "classics", in their own time they were the populist equivalent of today's TV soap operas. Even people who couldn't read knew all the latest stories, because it became the fashion for those who could read to read out loud to others. So, in big houses, the leading servants – such as the butler – would often read the latest "blockbuster" aloud to the under servants. In largely illiterate communities, the local vicar, teacher or doctor might hold weekly readings of the latest chapter of whichever popular novel was sweeping the nation.

As the education system improved and increasing numbers of people became literate, the publishing industry grew even more important and authors became the new celebrities. Charles Dickens went on modern-style book tours, travelling through Europe and to America and Canada; he was even planning a reading tour of Australia (where two of his sons were living) but he died before he could arrange it.

As a whole, Victorian literature became much more earnest than the literature of the previous few decades. Many of the famed Victorian writers were also passionately involved in social campaigning, and their novels and short stories reflected this zeal. It was an effective way of bringing about social change.

> *We have become a novel-reading people, from the Prime Minister down to the last-appointed scullery maid.*
> **Anthony Trollope, 1870**

THE ORIGIN OF SPECIES

On 24 November 1859, a book was published that caused a furore. *The Origin of Species* by Charles Darwin explained the scientist's groundbreaking theory: evolution. The book's full title was *On the Origin of Species by Means of Natural Selection, or the Preservation of Favoured Races in the Struggle for Life*. The book and Darwin's theories split Victorian society between the sciences and the Church. Evolution challenged the long-held Christian belief of how the world was created and Darwin's work caused many Christians to start questioning their faith.

Practise writing as an art. Study it as you would painting or music.

W.T. Stead, journalist and editor of *The Pall Mall Gazette*

THE RISE OF DETECTIVE FICTION

The Victorian era saw the rise of a new genre of literature: detective fiction. Charles Dickens's earliest writing about the police was a witty mention in *The Pickwick Papers*. He also wrote scathingly of police methods in *Oliver Twist*, but it was in *Martin Chuzzlewit* that he produced his first proper detective, Mr Nadgett, "a short, dried up, withered old man". He continued this theme in *Bleak House*, in which he introduced Inspector Bucket – a thinly veiled portrait of Dickens's detective friend Inspector Field – to solve a murder. Bucket is interesting because he is able to move with confidence amongst people from all areas of society, from baronets to criminals. One of the novel's characters, Mr Snagsby, describes him as "Detective Mr Bucket with his forefinger, and his confidential manner impossible to be evaded or declined". Mrs Bucket, his wife, is also a sleuth, much like that famous twentieth-century invention, Agatha Christie's Miss Marple.

In 1868, 15 years after Dickens published *Bleak House*, his friend Wilkie Collins published *The Moonstone*, often described as the first British detective novel. Both Dickens and Collins were fans of the American author Edgar Allan Poe, who had written *The Murders in the Rue Morgue* in 1841, shortly before his death.

This type of literature had really struck gold and immediately the appetite for "sensation novels" became insatiable. Adventure novels, stories of heroines in distress, and plots in which sensational secrets were revealed became immensely fashionable. Newspapers and magazines carried regular serials of mystery stories. In 1888, the novelist Reginald Barrett published a police story, *Police-Sergeant C21*. One of the most popular novelists of adventure fiction was Robert Louis Stevenson, whose novella *The Strange Case of Dr Jekyll and Mr Hyde* introduced a whole new breed of gothic fiction.

The most famous Victorian writer of detective fiction was Arthur Conan Doyle, the inventor of Sherlock Holmes. He was astounded by the success of his works and by how many people thought that his fictional character was a real person. The first story to introduce Sherlock Holmes and Doctor Watson was *A Study in Scarlet; Conan Doyle wrote the story in just three weeks and Sherlock mania was born*. When Conan Doyle killed off his character in 1893, in *The Final Problem*, the country was so shocked and the outcry so continuous that the author was later persuaded to bring him back to life.

> *The world is full of obvious things which nobody by any chance ever observes.*
>
> From *The Hound of the Baskervilles* by Arthur Conan Doyle, 1902

PENNY DREADFULS

The Victorian appetite for cheap, sensationalized fiction – the gorier the better – was seemingly insatiable. A publishing phenomenon of the nineteenth century was the Penny Dreadful. These were cheap magazines that related stories of murder, adventure and gothic terror. The text was accompanied by lurid illustrations, made even more dramatic by the use of colour printing.

THE CLIQUE

In 1837, a group of friends – all students at the Royal Academy in London – formed a new artistic group, which became known as The Clique. The intention was to improve their work and to concentrate on subjects they were all interested in, such as history and literature. The artists were Augustus Leopold Egg, William Powell Frith, Richard Dadd, Henry Nelson O'Neill, Alfred Elmore and John Phillip. Egg, Frith and Dadd were the most proactive of the group and at one point attempted to set up a new group; this was for artists whose works had been rejected by the Royal Academy and was intended to show opposition to the Academy. It was not a success; its only result was for the group to become nicknamed The Malcontents.

Frith remains the most famous of the group, particularly for his intricately detailed paintings *Derby Day* and *Railway Station*, and his portrait of his good friend Charles Dickens. Augustus Egg, who was also a close friend of Dickens, is best known for his socially conscious series of paintings, *Past and Present*, which show the downfall of a middle-class woman into poverty and despair after her husband discovers her adultery. In the series, Egg was able to show his distaste for the double standards of Victorian Britain, a country in which women were firmly third-class citizens, considered only after men and boys.

The most notorious of the group was Richard Dadd. He had been a child prodigy and his work as a fairy painter – a very popular type of art in early Victorian Britain – was hailed as some of the most original and exciting new artwork on the market. His paintings are minutely detailed, his most famous being one of his earliest paintings, *Puck* (1840), and *The Fairy-Feller's Master Stroke* (1855–64). In 1843, when he was in his late twenties, he returned from a painting trip through Europe and the Middle East, his normal happy and gentle personality seemingly very altered. His friends and family grew increasingly concerned and his father took him out for a walk in the fields one evening to talk to him. It was a fatal mistake as Dadd was carrying a weapon and stabbed his father repeatedly, then attempted to flee the country. He had made it as far as France when he got into a fight with a fellow passenger on a coach and attacked him with a razor; this led to his arrest and subsequent return to Britain. He was tried for murder and declared criminally insane. Dadd was committed to the Bethlem Asylum where he painted the pictures he has become most famous for. It is believed that he, as well as at least one of his siblings, suffered from schizophrenia. Dadd's brother George was also sent to the Bethlem Asylum and their sister Maria ended her life in another asylum.

THE PRE-RAPHAELITE BROTHERHOOD (PRB)

In the autumn of 1848, three young men gathered in a studio in central London, intent on forming a secret society to change the face of English art forever. As students at London's Royal Academy, the artists had grown frustrated with strict rules. Even long after his death, the dictates of the RA's first president, Sir Joshua Reynolds (1723–92), continued to be enforced. These three young men were John Everett Millais, Dante Gabriel Rossetti and William Holman Hunt. They asked four more friends to join them: Thomas Woolner, Frederic George Stephens, James Collinson and William Michael Rossetti.

The seven friends, all aged between 19 and 23, wanted to move art away from the sombre colour palettes, fixed subject matter and rigid conventions it was currently expected to adhere to. All were admirers of early Italianate art and they wanted to return English art to a freer, more experimental time. It is often claimed that they detested the work of the Italian Renaissance artist Raphael (1483–1520), but they actually admired many of his works – they were simply bored with being told that his was the only style to emulate. The problem was that Raphael had been so influential that it had become fashionable for all artists to follow his style. This did not allow for any breakthroughs or originality, and art had been allowed to stagnate. The Royal Academy, following the lead set by Joshua Reynolds, held up Raphael as an example to all artists; the members of this secret society decided it was time for a change.

Believing that art had "gone wrong" with Raphael, the young men named themselves the Pre-Raphaelite Brotherhood. They kept their new society secret to all but close friends, and began to sign their art not only with their signatures but also the initials "PRB". The idea for the Brotherhood came from Dante Rossetti, whose parents were Italian and whose political-refugee father had told him tales of the Carbonari, the Illuminati and other secret societies. The inaugural meeting was held at Millais's family home on Gower Street, in his basement studio. Of the seven, only six were artists. William Rossetti, younger brother of Dante, was an aspiring writer and artist, with a full-time day job at the tax office.

Like the eighteenth-century Romantic artists, the PRB were passionate about literature as well as art. They drew up a list of "immortals", which included artists, writers, philosophers, politicians, explorers and Jesus Christ (Thomas Woolner was very religious and insisted that Jesus be placed at the top of the list). They produced a monthly magazine, *The Germ: Thoughts towards Nature in Poetry, Literature and Art*. Dante Rossetti, James Collinson and the sculptor Thomas Woolner published their poetry in it. The magazine was expensive to produce and, at a hefty price of one shilling, was a financial disaster; very few copies were sold and only four issues were produced. Although a financial failure, it was critically acclaimed and, in later years, would be recognized as hugely influential.

The PRB only lasted for five years, but these were extremely significant. It came to an end when Thomas Woolner, the only sculptor in the group, decided to travel to Australia to attempt to make his fortune in the gold rush. The Pre-Raphaelite movement continued into the twentieth century.

This short-lived brotherhood remains one of the most influential of all English artistic rebellions. Of the original members, Millais, Holman Hunt and Dante Rossetti became some of the most famous and wealthy artists in Victorian England.

PRE-RAPHAELITE PRINCIPLES

At their first meeting, the Pre-Raphaelite Brotherhood came up with a set of four artistic principles:

1. To have genuine ideas to express.
2. To study nature attentively, so as to know how to express them.
3. To sympathize with what is direct and serious and heartfelt in previous art, to the exclusion of what is conventional and self-parading and learned by rote.
4. And most indispensable of all, to produce thoroughly good pictures and statues.

THE ARTS AND CRAFTS MOVEMENT

One of the most influential figures behind the Arts and Crafts movement was the designer, artist and Utopian Socialist William Morris (1834–96). As well as being an artist, William Morris was a campaigning Socialist, calling for equality for all. He wanted his new artistic movement to be about striving for basic human rights and dignity, as well as producing great art. William Morris was also a writer and, in addition to producing political pamphlets and manifestoes, he wrote a Utopian novel, *News from Nowhere* (1890).

The name of the new movement grew out of the Arts and Crafts Exhibition of 1888, in which Morris and many of his protégés had taken part. He wanted to bring back the artistic practices that were being lost in the mass production of post-Industrial-Revolution Britain. Morris encouraged artists and artisans to work on the types of crafts that seemed about to be lost to Britain forever. These included books –

especially illuminated manuscripts, the most famous of which is Morris's acclaimed *Kelmscott Chaucer* – wallpaper, furniture design, hand-dyed textiles, handmade fashion, embroidery, woodcarving, woodturning, gilding and architecture. He and his lifelong friend and fellow artist Edward Burne Jones were instrumental in bringing back into fashion the long-neglected art of tapestry.

Morris set up several companies including modern mills – run on fair principles – at Merton Abbey, south of London. His companies paid their workers fair wages for the work they produced, which was still a radical idea. Morris's dream was to make beautiful items that everyone could afford to buy, but the flaw in his plan was that, by paying his workers fairly and ensuring safe and happy working conditions, he could not afford to produce the cheap items that the mass manufacturers could.

The Arts and Crafts movement also spread to encompass architecture, and the very first Arts and Crafts home was created for William Morris and his wife, Janey (née Burden), at Bexleyheath in Kent. The house was designed jointly by William Morris and the architect Philip Webb. Morris's famous mantra was, "Have nothing in your houses that you do not know to be useful, or believe to be beautiful". He practised this in his own home. Above the door is carved the motto *Ars Longa Vita Brevis* (art endures but life is brief).

OTHER IMPORTANT ARTISTIC MOVEMENTS IN VICTORIAN BRITAIN

Aestheticism • Classicism • Decadence • The Glasgow Boys • The Glasgow School • Gothic Revival • The New English Art Club • Orientalism • Realism and Symbolism

---

THE GROSVENOR GALLERY

In 1877, the art world was agog with the news that a new art gallery was opening, one that was being created along Aesthetic lines – from its architecture to the art on its walls. It was intended to be a whole new artistic world to rival the fusty conventionality of the Royal Academy.

The gallery was heralded as a much-needed saviour of modern artists. Oscar Wilde attended the opening dressed in a new coat, specially commissioned for the opening night, which was shaped like the body of a cello. He made headlines all over the country. Every artist of note was there, including Princess Louise, an Aesthetic sculptor and lover of one of the most famous sculptors in the country, Joseph Edgar Boehm. Wilde wrote an article about the concept of the Grosvenor Gallery:

> *The origin of this Gallery is as follows: About a year ago the idea occurred to Sir Coutts Lindsay of building a public gallery, in which, untrammelled by the difficulties or meannesses of "Hanging Committees", he could exhibit to the lovers of art the works of certain great living artists side by side: a gallery in which the student would not have to struggle through an endless monotony of mediocre works in order to reach what was worth looking at; one in which the people of England could have the opportunity of judging of the merits of at least one great master of painting, whose pictures had been kept from public exhibition by the jealousy and ignorance of rival artists.*

THE RUSKIN V. WHISTLER CASE

In 1877, James Abbott McNeill Whistler exhibited his *Nocturne in Black and Gold: The Falling Rocket* at the Grosvenor Gallery. When the art critic John Ruskin visited the exhibition, he was incensed by what was, for the time, a very abstract painting. He published a scathing review of Whistler's work in which he wrote: "I have seen and heard much of Cockney impudence before now; but never expected to hear a coxcomb ask two hundred guineas for flinging a pot of paint in the public's face." Whistler sued Ruskin for libel, claiming his "reputation as an artist has been much damaged by the said libel". This case divided the Victorian art world, as both men were so well known and so influential.

In 1878, the case was heard at the Old Bailey. Ruskin's health was extremely poor at the time so his doctor declared him unfit to appear in court. These health problems were chiefly emotional and not physical – his mental health was deteriorating rapidly, possibly a sign of dementia. The artist Edward Burne-Jones was asked to appear in Ruskin's place, which he found excruciating as he was also friendly with Whistler. As agreed with his legal team, he said in court that the painting was a "failure" in its effort to recreate night and that he did not consider it worth 200 guineas. When cross-examined, however, he was compelled to comment, "Whistler had an almost unrivalled appreciation of atmosphere, and that his colour was beautiful, especially in moonlight scenes," which seemed to give the lie to his earlier comments.

When Whistler was asked how long it took him to paint, he replied that it only took a couple of days. He was then questioned as to why he was asking 200 guineas for it. His iconic answer spoke for all artists: "I ask it for the knowledge I have gained in the work of a lifetime."

The trial lasted for two days, with scores of London artists giving evidence, both for and against Whistler. The newspapers had a field day and the trial lead to a widespread discussion about the meaning and value of art, and whether it should have a moral or didactic purpose. Whistler was one of the most famous exponents of Aestheticism, an artistic movement whose motto was "Art for Art's Sake". Unlike earlier movements, Aestheticism did not require art to be campaigning or didactic, it simply needed to be beautiful.

Whistler won the court case, but there was humiliation to come. He had claimed for £1000 in damages, plus court costs, yet he was awarded only a farthing in damages and as he had still to pay his own costs, he ended up declaring himself bankrupt. Both Whistler and Ruskin were affected by the trial as anger rankled in the art world for many years, haunting both of them. Whistler was not able to sell his previously popular *Nocturnes* for some years to come and Ruskin was judged malicious and derided for being too cowardly to appear in court. The trial may have lasted only two days, but its repercussions and furious arguments raged through the art world for years. The press both judged Ruskin harshly and criticized Whistler's work and his arrogant attitude. Neither man won.

THEATRE

At the start of the nineteenth century, theatre in Britain needed a revolution. In the Victorian age, it happened. Far more theatres began to be built and travelling theatre companies traversed the country, taking plays and performances all over Britain.

At the start of Victoria's reign, it was common for nights at the theatre to contain more than one play, usually a serious play followed by a comedy or burlesque. By the end of her reign, theatres had become increasingly centred around more sophisticated plays and burlesque had moved into the music halls, where all manner of variety shows could be seen.

Theatre was for all social classes. The wealthy took seats in the theatre boxes, all of which were intentionally positioned for observing the rest of the audience as well as the stage. The cheapest theatre tickets were for places in the "pit", where people stood or sat on the ground. By the end of the nineteenth century, the theatre had become much more accessible for the middle classes.

In 1843, a new Act of Parliament was passed, ending the monopoly enjoyed by the few most influential theatres and acting dynasties. The new act allowed all theatres to stage serious plays, such as Shakespeare – this was something that had previously been the province of only the top theatres. In London, just two theatres had enjoyed that privilege: the Covent Garden Theatre and the Drury Lane Theatre.

> *I thought I would afterwards go to the play. The theatre where Mr Wopsle had achieved his questionable triumph, was in that waterside neighbourhoods (it is nowhere now), and to that theatre I resolved to go. I was aware that Mr Wopsle had not succeeded in reviving the Drama, but, on the contrary, had rather partaken of its decline.*
>
> **From *Great Expectations* by Charles Dickens, 1860**

GREAT NAMES OF THE VICTORIAN STAGE

The two most popular actors in Victorian Britain were Henry Irving (1838–1905) and Ellen Terry (1847–1928). Both would receive honours from the monarch (he became a knight, she a dame), and were credited with making the theatre respectable.

Ellen Terry was born into an acting family and made her stage debut at the age of eight (she was actually nine but her father lied about her age to make her seem more of a child prodigy, and Ellen believed for her entire life that she was a year younger than she actually was). To be a child, especially a female child, on the stage at that time was fraught with dangers. Girls were often expected to wear very revealing costumes, supposedly because they were so young and "innocent", which left them open to the attentions of paedophiles. It was a hard-working life, but for Ellen Terry it was the life she had always known.

Henry Irving grew up outside the theatre, but longed to enter it. His parents were strict Methodists and discouraged his love of acting; it took him many long years to be taken seriously. He worked as a jobbing bit-part actor for over a decade and a half, struggling to cope financially, and was in his late thirties before he found sudden success, after his performance in a play entitled *The Bells*. According to legend, on the night of his great success and what he hoped (correctly) would be the start of a glittering career, he was in a carriage with his wife on their way home when she asked him when he was going to give up his nonsensical theatrical dreams. Irving later said that he instantly stopped the carriage, stepped out onto the road, and never went home again. It was rumoured that he and Ellen Terry were lovers for many years, as well as being business partners in the most successful actor-manager duo in Britain.

Ellen Terry lived her life in a very unconventional manner. She did everything a Victorian woman was not expected to do – yet she had such charisma and talent that she managed to remain accepted, adored and respected. Even the usually censorious Queen Victoria admired her work. Terry's first marriage was at the age of 16 (actually 17) to the painter G. F. Watts, who was 45. The marriage was unconsummated and after 11 months he sent her home to her parents. She then lived with the Aesthetic architect E. W. Godwin, with whom she had two children before he left her to marry an heiress. Following that, she made a brief second marriage to the actor Charles Kelly, before she discovered he was an alcoholic and divorced him. In 1907, at the age of 59 (60), she married a 31-year-old American actor named James Carew.

Censorship. The person who controlled the theatre's morals was the British Lord Chamberlain. His job was to ensure that there was no nudity, lewdness or lack of "decorum" in plays, and also that they proved no threat to the "public peace" nor risked inciting political unrest.

5

LEISURE TIME

Although many Victorians remained poor throughout the Queen's reign, there were others who rose through the social ranks and benefitted from the luxury of having increased leisure time. Entrepreneurs were keen to take advantage of this. Popular activities included visiting public parks and stately homes (whose owners were starting to realize the need to make money from their property), taking afternoon tea, dining at smart restaurants, and visiting music halls, the theatre and the opera. At the start of Victoria's reign, the social lives of women were greatly restricted since many public activities were considered unsuitable for them; however, by the end of the nineteenth century, this had changed dramatically.

PLEASURE GARDENS

During the seventeenth and eighteenth centuries, one of the most popular public attractions was the pleasure gardens of London. There were three major gardens: Vauxhall, Marylebone and Ranelagh. By the Victorian age, Ranelagh and Marylebone had closed, and Vauxhall had become less splendid and more shabby. While Casanova and Oliver Goldsmith had written with awe about the wonders within, by the time the young Charles Dickens visited in the 1830s, he was disappointed by Vauxhall's faded splendour. In the 1840s, the new Cremorne Gardens were opened in Chelsea. One of their regular visitors was the artist James Abbott McNeill Whistler, who lived nearby and was inspired to paint it.

PLEASURE GARDEN FACTS

- The Vauxhall pleasure gardens opened in *c.*1661 and were originally known as "New Spring Gardens". The gardens closed in 1859, after losing much of their audience to more modern forms of entertainment, such as the music halls.
- The initial success of the London pleasure gardens inspired entrepreneurs to create them elsewhere. By the start of Queen Victoria's reign, several gardens were thriving in cities including Bristol, Liverpool, Birmingham, Manchester and Norwich.

"Skittles" is another favourite amusement, and the coster-mongers class themselves among the best players in London. The game is always for beer, but betting goes on. A fondness for "sparring" and "boxing" lingers among the rude members of some classes of the working men, such as the tanners. With the great majority of the costermongers, this fondness is still as dominant as it was among the "higher classes", when boxers were the pets of princes and nobles. The sparring among the costers is not for money, but for beer and a "lark" – a convenient word covering much mischief. Two out of every ten landlords, whose houses are patronised by these lovers of "the art of self-defence" supply gloves. Some charge 2d a night for their use; others only 1d. The sparring seldom continues long, sometimes not above a quarter of an hour.

From **London Labour and the London Poor** by **Henry Mayhew**, 1851

BANK HOLIDAYS

- The name "bank holiday" derives from the days on which the banks were closed for business.
- In 1834, the banks decided on just four days a year when they would be closed: 1 May, 1 November, Good Friday (which is moveable every year, dependent on the date of Easter) and Christmas Day (25 December).

- There had been discussion for many years about creating more public holidays – in 1871 an Act of Parliament was passed, which had been proposed by a banker named Sir John Lubbock. This decreed that bank holidays should be a holiday for every worker.
- After the Act was passed, there was continuing discussion as to which days should be holidays in the different countries within the British Isles. The intention was for the holidays – when possible – to fall on a Monday.
- For a few years, bank holidays were referred to as "St Lubbock's Days". Sir John Lubbock was a mad-keen cricketer and there were rumours that the reason he proposed so many spring and summer dates was so that he could arrange more cricket matches.
- Although bank holidays were a new idea for the Victorians, they had close connections with days which had long been celebrated in Britain by annual fairs or religious festivities, dating back to early Christian or pagan times.

THE ARRIVAL OF THE WEEKEND

In 1843, the doctor and social campaigner William Marsden fought for workers in the cotton mills of Manchester to have a half-day off work every Saturday. At that time, labourers worked six days a week, and their only day off was Sunday. Strict religious laws made the pursuit of most leisure pursuits impossible on this day. Marsden's campaign was hugely popular and the concept of a "half-day Saturday" soon spread around the country. The now traditional Saturday afternoon football match and other sports fixtures date from this period.

The use of the word "weekend" was first noted by the *Oxford English Dictionary* in 1879, but it was not in common use until the early twentieth century. By the end of the nineteenth century, it had become popular for country house parties to take place over the "weekend", but most working-class people still worked on Saturday mornings. The new half-day Saturday did not usually apply to household servants, instead they were given a half day at a time in the week that suited their employers.

VICTORIAN CHRISTMASES

When Prince Albert married Queen Victoria, he brought Germanic Christmas traditions with him. For several generations, the royal family had celebrated by bringing a tree into the house and decorating it with candles and baubles, but the practice was little known elsewhere in the country. In the 1840s, Prince Albert allowed newspapers to publish illustrations of the family's Christmas tree and decorations. Following the publication of an engraving of the royal family with their Christmas tree in 1848, Christmas trees started to appear across the country.

In 1843 – the same year that Charles Dickens's *A Christmas Carol* was published – the first Christmas card was produced. It was commissioned and sent out by Henry Cole, a civil servant (later one of the main forces behind the Great Exhibition of 1851 and the first director of the South Kensington museums). The card, designed by J. C. Horsley, showed a family celebrating Christmas together and raising their glasses in a toast.

In 1848, a British confectioner named Tom Smith was inspired to sell his products in a new style he had seen in Paris. After seeing French *bonbons* wrapped up in twists of paper, he decided to do the same for his confectionery in time for Christmas. The idea proved very popular and Smith's invention was the very first Christmas cracker.

Victorian Christmas did not have the extended period of preparation or commercialism of today. Christmas began on 24 December and continued until 6 January, Twelfth Night. The night of 5 January through to the morning of 6 January was a big Victorian celebration for which people held parties, danced, sang and ate "Twelfth Cake" – a rich fruit cake. In 1870, Queen Victoria ordered that celebration of Twelfth Night be banned, considering the festival unruly and pagan. Too many newspapers had reported tricks played by "urchins", such as putting firecrackers through people's doors.

During Queen Victoria's reign, Christmas was not a bank holiday and the vast majority of people did not get the day off work. The expression "Boxing Day" derives from the nineteenth century: 26 December was the date on which servants were given a day off, in recompense for their hard work over Christmas. The word "boxing" has nothing to do with sports – it was the day on which servants, delivery boys and tradespeople were given their "Christmas box", usually a present of money.

TWELFTH CAKE RECIPE

This celebratory cake was elaborately decorated with icing, sugar figures, paper patterns, flowers and ribbons. Hidden inside the cake were a dried pea and a dried bean. Whoever found the dried bean in their slice of cake was the king for the evening (or if a woman got the bean she elected a man to be king), and whoever found the pea was the elected queen (or, if a man got it, he chose a woman to be queen).

Take seven pounds of flour, make a cavity in the centre, set a sponge with a gill and a half of yeast and a little warm milk; then put round it one pound of fresh butter broke into small lumps, one pound and a quarter of sifted sugar, four pounds and a half of currants washed and picked, half an ounce of sifted cinnamon, a quarter of an ounce of pounded cloves, mace, and nutmeg mixed, sliced candied orange or lemon peel and citron. When the sponge is risen, mix all the ingredients together with a little warm milk; let the hoops be well papered and buttered, then fill them with the mixture and bake them, and when nearly cold, ice them over with sugar prepared for that purpose as per receipt; or they may be plain.

From *The Art of Cookery Made Easy and Refined*
by John Mollard, 1808

CHRISTMAS RECIPES

Plum Pudding
Mrs Beeton's Book of Household Management contained over 2,000 recipes, including many Christmas recipes.

Plum Pudding (for 10 people)
5 ozs of breadcrumbs, 4 ozs of flour, 4 ozs of finely chopped suet, 4 ozs of raisins, halved and stoned, 4 ozs of currants, washed and dried, 4 ozs of moist sugar, 2 ozs of shredded candied peel, 2 ozs of raw carrot grated, 1 level teaspoonful of finely grated lemon-

rind, $^1/_2$ a saltspoonful of grated nutmeg, 1 good teaspoonful of baking-powder, about $^1/_4$ of a pint of milk, 2 eggs. Mix all the dry ingredients except the baking-powder together, add the beaten eggs and sufficient milk to thoroughly moisten the whole, then cover, and let the mixture stand for 1 hour. When ready, stir in baking-powder, turn into a buttered mould or basin, and boil for 6 hours, or steam for 7 hours. Serve with a suitable sauce.

Plum Pudding Sauce
$^1/_4$ of a pint of milk, 2 glasses of brandy, 1 tablespoonful of castor sugar, the yolks of 2 eggs, a very little grated lemon-rind.
Mix all the ingredients in a saucepan, set the pan on the fire, and whisk until the contents thicken and become frothy. Serve at once.

A CHRISTMAS CAROL

In the autumn of 1843, Charles Dickens travelled to Manchester for a special fundraising dinner at the city's new Athenaeum Club. His fellow speakers included Benjamin Disraeli and Richard Cobden. The club's mission, to provide adult education for the city's workers, was one that Dickens felt passionate about. The Industrial Revolution was well underway and Manchester was experiencing a financial boom – but not everyone was reaping the results. The novelist thought he had experienced poverty in London, but he was unprepared for the misery he would witness that cold Manchester autumn. He returned to London determined "to strike a hammer blow in favour of the poor man's child". After six weeks he had written a novella entitled *A Christmas Carol*.

Dickens's publishers had been unhappy with the sales of his previous novel, *Martin Chuzzlewit*, and had been loath to back the author's idea of a Christmas novella, so Dickens paid for the majority of the costs himself. He published *A Christmas Carol* in December 1843, with an initial print run of 6,000 copies. These sold out within five days.

The time draws near the birth of Christ;
The moon is hid; the night is still;
The Christmas bells from hill to hill
Answer each other in the mist.

From "In Memoriam" by Alfred, Lord Tennyson

To bring about a general feeling of enjoyment, much depends
on the surroundings… It is worth while to bestow some little
trouble on the decoration of the rooms.

Cassell's Family Magazine, 1881

AFTERNOON TEA

The fashion for afternoon tea was created by one of Queen Victoria's ladies-in-waiting, Anna, the 7th Duchess of Bedford. As the normal time for eating dinner was becoming later in the evening, the duchess famously commented that she was tired of "having that sinking feeling" in the middle of the afternoon. So, in 1840, she began asking her servants to bring her a pot of tea, and a plate of bread and butter. Soon she was inviting her friends to join her and the practice spread. Initially, it was a simple, light snack followed by a walk, but Queen Victoria was an early fan of afternoon tea and, as she had a very sweet tooth, it became the fashion to enjoy cakes as well. By the end of the nineteenth century, afternoon tea had become an elaborate and much larger meal, as well as an accepted part of a woman's day. Teashops and hotels were quick to take advantage of the new craze.

VICTORIA SPONGE

In 1861, Mrs Beeton published the first known recipe for what she called "Victoria Sandwiches", but which is better known today as a Victoria Sponge. This was named after the monarch, as it was the type of sweet sponge cake that the Queen was known to love.

Ingredients:
4 eggs; their weight in pounded sugar, butter and flour
$\frac{1}{4}$ saltspoonful of salt,
a layer of any kind of jam or marmalade.
Mode: *Beat the butter to a cream; dredge in the flour and pounded*
sugar; stir these ingredients well together, and add the eggs, which
should be previously thoroughly whisked. When the mixture has
been well beaten for about 10 minutes, butter a Yorkshire-pudding
tin, pour in the batter, and bake it in a moderate oven for 20
minutes. Let it cool, spread one half of the cake with a layer of nice
preserve, place over it the other half of the cake, press the pieces
slightly together, and then cut it into long finger-pieces; pile them in
cross bars on a glass dish, and serve.
Time: *20 minutes.*
Average cost, 1s 3d.
Sufficient for 5 or 6 persons. Seasonable at any time.

MUSIC HALLS

Throughout the nineteenth century, people would visit inns and taverns expecting to see variety acts and popular singers, and pubs started to attach makeshift theatres to the main building. In 1843, a newly passed Theatre Act began to crack down on these unofficial theatres, and withheld licences to sell alcohol from those that didn't have an official entertainment licence. The resulting boom in official – and licensed – places of entertainment saw the creation of the music hall. The very first music halls appeared in the London suburbs, but they had soon spread across the country. By the 1870s, there were nearly 400 music halls throughout Britain.

In past times, going to the theatre had been considered an upper-class luxury, but the music halls were much cheaper to attend and open to everyone. Popular music hall performers included Sam Cowell, Charles Sloman, George Robey, Wilkie Bard, Harry Champion, G. H. Elliott, Florrie Forde, George Lashwood, Dan Leno and Marie Lloyd. Many women found fame on the music hall stage as male impersonators, including Vesta Tilley and the American star Ella Shields, best remembered for her song "Burlington Bertie from Bow". The most successful music hall singers wrote their own songs which became famous, and for which sheet music and lyrics were sold on the streets so people could play them at home. The artist Walter Sickert was fascinated by music halls, and began painting the buildings, performers and audiences. His paintings provide a detailed record of what it was like to enter a Victorian music hall.

DANCING

Many celebrations in Victorian Britain centred on dancing, from simple country dances to grand balls. Dances were held for weddings, birthdays and christenings. On Mayday, the traditional dance around the maypole could be seen at fairs all over the country – this dates back to an ancient ceremony that welcomed the coming of summer. Dances were also held on Twelfth Night (the night of 5–6 January) to mark the last day of Christmas.

One of the most popular dances of the early Victorian era was the polka, which had originated in Bohemia and swept Britain's dance floors in the 1840s. Other popular dances included the waltz, the mazurka, the gallop and the two-step. Dancing was a very important part of social life and those who could afford it hired dancing teachers to ensure their children would equip themselves well in society. The most fashionable dance teachers often created new dances or dance steps to increase their celebrity.

Dancing fashions and etiquette were strictly observed, and unmarried young women could only attend a dance in the company of an eagle-eyed chaperone (usually an older woman). Women in mourning were not permitted to dance, and in the earliest stages of mourning they did not attend social events at all.

As Queen Victoria's love of Scotland increased, Scottish dancing became fashionable all over Britain. Conversely, other traditional forms of country and folk dancing, from regions in Wales, Ireland and England, had declined in popularity by the time of Victoria's reign.

In the late Victorian period, a popular high-society event was the fancy dress ball, held by the wealthy, the glamorous and the more bohemian members of the royal family. Attendees wore elaborate costumes that had taken weeks to make – appearing as figures from history, such as Marie-Antoinette or Dante Alighieri – and photographers were commissioned to record them for posterity.

6

THE INDUSTRIAL REVOLUTION

The Industrial Revolution, which began in earnest in the eighteenth century, changed the British Isles forever. By the middle of Queen Victoria's reign, the main employers in Britain were based in urban areas and were involved in industry and manufacturing. As the population's expectations and needs changed, politicians had to start introducing changes to the way people were treated, specifically in the world of work.

POLITICAL CHANGES

The 1833 Factory Act banned children under the age of nine from working in textile factories and limited the working hours of older children. Nine-to-13-year-olds could only work for a maximum of nine hours in a day and 48 hours in a week, and 13-to-18-year-olds could only work for a maximum of 12 hours in a day and 69 hours in a week. The Act also specified that all children under 11 were to have at least two hours of education a day. The new law was enforced by government factory inspectors.

The 1842 Mines and Collieries Act banned women and all children under the age of 10 from working underground. It also prohibited anyone under the age of 15 from operating the mines' dangerous "winding gear".

The 1844 Factory Act changed the minimum working age for working in a factory to eight years old. Eight-to-13-year-olds could now only work six and a half hours on weekdays and six hours on Saturdays, and 13-to-18-year-olds could work a maximum of 12 hours a day. Women could work a maximum of 12 hours a day.

The 1847 Fielder's Factory Act introduced a maximum 10-hour working day for women and children under the age of 18.

The 1864 Factory Act extended the regulations to all factories (the initial factory acts were concerned only with textile factories and coalmines).

VICTORIAN INVENTIONS THAT CHANGED THE WORLD

- 1837 – the telegraph machine, Samuel Morse
- 1837 – the postage stamp, Rowland Hill
- 1843 – the *SS Great Britain*, Isambard Kingdom Brunel
- 1843 – the Thames Tunnel, Marc Brunel and Isambard Kingdom Brunel
- 1865 – the Bessemer Converter, Henry Bessemer
- 1876 – the telephone, Alexander Graham Bell
- 1885 – the motor car, Karl Benz

HENRIETTA VANSITTART (NÉE LOWE) (1833–83)

Several women were pivotal in the Industrial Revolution although their names have been almost entirely forgotten. Henrietta Vansittart was a lower-middle-class woman and the daughter of impoverished parents who became respected in the engineering world because of her inventions. Henrietta's father, James Lowe, invented the marine screw propeller; following his death in 1866, Henrietta continued his work and improved the design. She was granted a patent in 1868 and, the following year, was invited by the Admiralty to give the propeller a trial on the ship HMS *Druid*. In honour of her father, Henrietta named her invention the Lowe-Vansittart propeller. It was still in use during the twentieth century, perhaps most famously as part of the ill-fated passenger ship the *Lusitania* (which was attacked and sunk during the First World War).

The inscription on James Lowe's grave memorial reads as follows:

Sacred to the memory of James Lowe, Esq., who was born May 13th 1798 and met his death from an accident the 12th October 1866. He was the Inventor of the Segment of the Screw Propeller in use since 1838 and his life though unobtrusive was not without great benefit to his country. He suffered many troubles but bore them lightly as his hope was not of this world but in our Saviour. Erected by his sorrowing Widow and his affectionate daughter, Henrietta Vansittart.

THE GREAT EXHIBITION

On 1 May 1851, Queen Victoria opened the Great Exhibition of the Works of Industry of all Nations (otherwise known as the Great Exhibition). For months, people walking in London's Hyde Park had been able to glimpse the site of an extraordinary new building project, a palace made of iron and glass – it contained over 4,000 tonnes of iron and an estimated one million feet (over 300 km) of glass. The design, by the master gardener and architect Sir Joseph Paxton, was constructed by over 2,000 workers and took just nine months to build. The architect did not just design the building but he also created innovative machines to help with its construction.

Two of Hyde Park's ancient trees were encased inside the vast area and the pink glass fountain in the middle of the construction reached a height of 27 feet (8 m) with ease. There were over 100,000 exhibits to explore from all over the world, including Persia, India and the Americas. For the first couple of weeks, admission prices were set at £3 for men and £2 for women, but at the end of May this changed to just a shilling a head, to ensure as any people as possible could visit.

There were an astonishing number of new inventions showcased in the exhibition, including printing machines (one of which could print 5,000 newspapers an hour), machines for adding figures, textiles from all over the world and inventions to help deaf and blind people – including a new type of ink that would remain raised from the paper when dry, so a blind person could feel the letters that had been written. Works of art

– including ceramics, tapestries and an entire wall of stained glass – were shown alongside experimental weapons. There was a machine for making cigarettes, exciting new designs for horse-drawn carriages, the latest locomotives and even a vast hydraulic press used for constructing bridges – which could be operated by just one man. Over 15,000 contributors brought their wares to the exhibition. Thrilled with the success of her husband's grand scheme, Queen Victoria commented, "The tremendous cheering, the joy expressed in every face, the vastness of the building, with all its decorations and exhibits, the sounds of the organ, and my beloved husband the creator of this great 'Peace Festival', uniting the industry and art of all nations of the earth was quite overwhelming."

⤴ The Crystal Palace was the first public building in Britain to offer "public conveniences", where for the price of a penny visitors could have the comfort of their own private cubicle. This is how the expression to "spend a penny" originated.

⤴ The Great Exhibition opened on 1 May 1851 and closed on 11 October 1851. During those months, more than six million visitors, of every social class and including visitors from all over the globe, queued to get inside the Crystal Palace.

GLASS AND IRON

When the Great Exhibition building committee held an architectural competition to find a suitable building, 248 plans were submitted and all were rejected. By May 1850, a year before the opening day, the committee were on the point of designing a building themselves. Joseph Paxton went to see the committee with a design he had sketched on a sheet of blotting paper. Instead of the usual bricks and mortar, he proposed a pre-fabricated building made of glass and iron.

The Birmingham manufacturer Chance Bros produced 300,000 panes of glass for construction of the Crystal Palace. The design was held together by 330 tall and thin cast-iron columns, and if the palace's gutters had been laid end to end they would have stretched for 24 miles (39 km).

...we find, first, the great Electric Clock; and next we notice clocks that will go for four hundred days with once winding up; watches that are so accurate from injury by damp, that they are exhibited suspended in water, and performing with regularity; a money-calculating machine, suited to the currency of all nations; an instrument for the solution of difficult problems in spherical trigonometry (obviously a great comfort)....We ought not to omit the mention of a few of the ingenious surgical inventions (and here our French exhibiters are most skilful) such as the artificial leech; apparatus and tools to meet the loss of the right hand; the artificial leg, to enable those who have lost that limb above the knee, to ride, walk, sit gracefully, or even dance; an illuminative instrument for inspecting the inside of the ear, and another for the eye; the guard razor, which shaves off hair, and will not cut flesh... and so on.

From "The Great Exhibition and the Little One" by Charles Dickens,
Household Words, 5 July 1851

JOSEPH PAXTON (1803–65)

Born in the town of Milton Bryan in Bedfordshire to a farming family, Joseph Paxton's first job was as a garden labourer. He became interested in landscaping very early in his career and at the age of 19 he created his first ornamental lake. In 1823, he found a job at the Horticultural Society's gardens in Chiswick; it was while working there that he first made the acquaintance of the Duke of Devonshire. The duke was so impressed that he offered him a job at his Derbyshire estate, Chatsworth. By his mid-twenties Paxton had been made chief gardener at Chatsworth and, despite having no architectural training, began designing greenhouses and landscaping the gardens. His greenhouses would later be his inspiration for the design of Crystal Palace.

After the success of the Great Exhibition, Paxton became a celebrity. He was knighted by Queen Victoria and everyone wanted him to design glasshouses for their gardens. His fortune was made and he began to think about a new career, in politics. In 1854, Paxton was elected Member of Parliament for Coventry, a position he held until his death. He died in 1865 in Sydenham on the outskirts of London.

THE BLANTYRE MINING DISASTER

At 8.45am on 22 October 1877, a devastating underground explosion tore through one of the coal mines at Blantyre Colliery in Scotland. Blantyre had five pits and produced hundreds of thousands of tons of coal every year. A few days previously, several miners had raised concerns about the levels of gas in the mines, but their complaints had been ignored.

Around 230 men had started work that morning at 5.30am, as usual. When the explosion was heard outside the mine, witnesses saw flames shooting out of the mine shafts numbered three and five. There was chaos as women rushed to the mine to see if their loved ones had survived. The rescue effort took over a week. There was great relief when four men were found alive, but they died of their injuries shortly afterwards. Not all bodies could be recovered, but the death toll was placed at over 215 men and boys. More than 250 children were left fatherless and 90 women widowed.

The mine was owned by William Dixon and Company, which also owned the workers' homes known as Dixon's Rows. Just a few months after the disaster, the community was shocked when widows and orphans of those killed were made homeless when they were turned out of Dixon's Rows to make way for the new workers.

A relief fund was set up for the miners' families, which raised over £8,000. The biggest individual donor was the philanthropist the 3rd Marquis of Bute, who gave £500. Another prominent donor was the banking heiress Angela Burdett-Coutts.

7

CRIME AND DETECTION

During the nineteenth century, police officers worked seven days a week, almost every week of the year, for which they were paid a guinea (one pound and one shilling) per week. Their holiday allowance was five days a year – and that was unpaid. Victorian police officers were carefully regulated to minimize the risk of corruption. They had to wear uniform at all times, even when off duty; this was because of a public fear about being spied on by someone without realizing he was a police officer.

POLICE FACTS

- In 1800, Scotland established its first police force, the City of Glasgow Police.
- In 1814, the Royal Irish Constabulary was founded.
- In 1829, the Metropolitan Police Force was founded in London.
- In 1830, following the death of William Huskisson on the Liverpool to Manchester Railway, the first railway police force was formed.
- The County Police Act was passed in 1839, bringing policing to all areas of England.

The primary object of an efficient police is the prevention of crime: the next that of detection and punishment of offenders if crime is committed. To these ends all the efforts of police must be directed. The protection of life and property, the

preservation of public tranquillity, and the absence of crime,
will alone prove whether those efforts have been successful
and whether the objects for which the police were appointed
have been attained.

Sir Richard Mayne (joint first Commissioner of the Metropolitan
Police), 1829

THE METROPOLITAN POLICE AND SIR ROBERT PEEL

In 1829, the first Metropolitan Police Act was passed under the auspices of the Home Secretary, Robert Peel. This led to the establishment of the Metropolitan Police Force, a replacement for the disorganized and often derided attempts to set up a police force in the past; it took in the river police, Bow Street Runners and other chaotic attempts to police the city.

Two commissioners were named: Colonel Charles Rowan and Richard Mayne, and they agreed that the primary duty of the police would be crime prevention. This left a huge gap in policing policy, namely the detection of crime and criminal behaviour. In 1842, this was remedied by the founding of the first Detective Department. Until this time, the "peelers" (as the police were known, in reference to Robert Peel) were still considered something of a joke, but the arrival of police detectives caught the public imagination and provided the media with sensational news stories. From 1842 onwards, the Metropolitan Police gained far more respect than any police force in Britain had previously been able to command.

- Sir Robert Peel died in the summer of 1850, following a riding accident on London's Constitution Hill. He suffered fatal injuries after being thrown from his horse.

- The British police have had two nicknames that derived from the name of Robert Peel: "peelers", which was in common use in the nineteenth century, and "bobbies", which came into usage some time later.

- Victorian police officers were forbidden to vote in elections.

TELEGRAPH ARREST

In 1845, a criminal was arrested for the first time thanks to the new telegraph technology. A telegraph message was sent from Slough to the police in London, alerting them to a suspected killer travelling by train. The suspect, John Tawell, was earmarked for arrest the minute he stepped off the train at Paddington Station. He was later convicted of murdering his former lover, the mother of his two illegitimate children. Her name was Sarah Hart, and she lived in Salt Hill, near Slough. Tawell was a pharmacist – when visiting Sarah, he took with him a medication that contained prussic acid. He managed to poison her beer and left. A neighbour saw him leaving and heard Sarah's groans. Another neighbour raced to the station and saw Tawell boarding the 7.42pm service to London. He was unable to stop the train, but gave a description to the police. Unfortunately for Tawell, Slough was one of the country's first train stations to be equipped with a telegraph machine.

When Sergeant William Williams received the message in London, he covered up his police uniform with a large coat and followed Tawell out of Paddington Station. Tawell boarded an omnibus and Williams trailed the man to his lodging house. Unfortunately, as soon as Tawell left the station grounds, Williams was powerless to arrest him: in the Victorian era, railway police had no jurisdiction outside railway property. So, after seeing where Tawell lived, Williams went to the local police station at Paddington Green and spoke to another police officer. The following morning the two policemen arrested Tawell at his local coffee house.

Tawell was hanged on 28 March 1845, after fully confessing to the prison chaplain. Around 10,000 people came to witness the execution.

MISSING Q

The telegraph machine was not equipped with the letter 'Q', which led to an odd spelling in the message sent from Slough. It read: "A murder has just been committed at Salt Hill and the suspected murderer was seen to take a first-class ticket to London by the train that left Slough at 7.42pm. He is in the garb of a Kwaker [*sic*] with a brown great coat on which reaches his feet. He is in the last compartment of the second first-class carriage."

⚑ In John Tawell's trial, his lawyer, Sir Fitzroy Kelly, attempted to persuade the jury that Sarah Hart's death had been caused by eating apples, because apple pips contain a tiny amount of prussic acid (more usually known today by the name cyanide). The sales of apples dipped sharply after reports of the trial appeared in newspapers.

⚑ The first trans-Atlantic telegraph cable was laid in 1866.

⚑ The railway police were provided with special station houses at regular intervals along railway lines. It is possible that the term "police station" is a legacy of these buildings.

SPRING-HEELED JACK

Throughout the nineteenth century, tales abounded of a terrifying figure who attacked women walking at night and even forced his way through doors and assaulted people in their homes. His nickname, as coined by the media, was "Spring-heeled Jack". The earliest sightings were in Sheffield at the very start of the 1800s. In some stories, he was described as having claws like a wild animal or eyes "like the devil", while in others, he was reputed to have spoken and looked like a man until he began his vicious attack. His nickname came from the fact that he was said to be able to bound away, as if on springs – some said he was able to leap onto rooftops and disappear into the night.

Spring-heeled Jack was credited with multiple and varied attacks all over the country, and then, in 1845, he was named as a murderer. His supposed victim was a child sex worker, 13-year-old Maria Davis, who had been killed on Jacob's Island, a notoriously dangerous part of east London.

By the 1870s, Spring-heeled Jack had become a favourite topic of sensationalist writers, appearing regularly in the Penny Dreadfuls and other magazines. By the 1880s, sightings of the monster abounded in the Black Country. In September 1886, the Birmingham Post reported "First a young girl, then a man, felt a hand on their shoulder, and turned to see the infernal one with glowing face, bidding them a good evening." His legend continued well into the twentieth century.

FAMOUS VICTORIAN MURDERS

- In April 1842, Daniel Good murdered his common-law wife, Jane Jones, dismembered her and attempted to burn her remains. Good was also a thief, and the murder was discovered by chance when a policeman was sent to his home to search for clothes he was alleged to have stolen. When the police arrived, Good fled and eluded capture for 10 days. This so shamed the Metropolitan Police – who were derided in the papers – that the new Detective Department was subsequently set up.

- In 1849, an unusual double execution took place at Horsemonger Lane Gaol. The couple who were executed were husband and wife, Maria and Frederick Mannings, and had been convicted of murdering Maria's wealthy lover, Patrick O'Connor, and stealing his belongings. The case caused a sensation and tour companies offered package trips to London to watch the execution take place. Much was made of the fact that Maria was Swiss and spoke with a French accent, which the newspapers seemed to think would make her a more likely murderer.

- In 1856, Dr William Palmer, a deeply indebted gambler, was executed for the murder of his wealthy friend John Cook, in 1855. Palmer had used strychnine to murder Cook and, although it was never proved, he is also suspected of having killed a number of other victims, including his brother, his wife's mother and four of his baby children. Palmer became known as the Rugeley Poisoner, after the town in which he lived.

- In 1860, 16-year-old Constance Kent was arrested for the brutal murder of her half-brother, Francis, aged four. His throat had been cut with a razor. As the newspapers followed the gruesome case and a famous London detective was sent to Rode, in Wiltshire, to investigate, opinions around the country were strongly divided as to whether or not Constance was guilty. In 1865, after a lengthy investigation and years in prison, Constance confessed to the crime and was sentenced to death. Her sentence was later commuted to life in prison. She was released in 1885, at the age of 41, and died in 1944 at the age of 100. After leaving prison, she refused to speak of the murder or to confirm or recant her confession.

- In March 1873, a woman dubbed the "black widow" was executed at Durham Gaol. Mary Ann Cotton had been married four times, and was convicted of poisoning three of her husbands to claim on their insurance policies. The poison she favoured was arsenic and, although it is unknown just how many people she killed, it has been speculated that the number could have been more than 20. Arsenic poisoning was often mistaken for gastric flu, a disease that could often prove fatal in Victorian Britain. Mary Ann gave birth to 13 children, of whom only two survived her. Her other possible victims included her stepchildren, friends and even her mother.

- In 1888, Britain was gripped by "Ripper-mania", horrified by the bloody reports from the East End of London of vicious serial killings. Who was the man the newspapers had dubbed "Jack the Ripper"? The mystery remains unsolved, although multiple names were suggested, including one of Queen Victoria's grandsons, Prince Eddy. It is unknown how many people the Ripper may have murdered in total, but there are five known victims with similar wounds and methods of murder. They were all female prostitutes who worked in or around the Whitechapel area of east London: Mary Ann Nichols, Annie Chapman, Elizabeth Stride, Catherine Eddowes and Mary Jane Kelly. The women were murdered between 31 August and 9 November 1888.

⤝ There were no female police officers in Britain in Queen Victoria's day. The Women's Police Service was not set up until 1914.

FOUNDING OF LOCAL POLICE FORCES

In 1856, the police began to carry truncheons. The initial police uniform was intended to make them look like other members of the public, so they wore frock coats over their trousers, and top hats on their heads – both of which proved impractical. In 1864, the police uniform was changed to a tunic and a helmet. Until the mid-1880s, policemen carried a large rattle made of wood so they could attract attention from other police if they needed assistance. In 1884, this was changed to a policeman's whistle.

8

POLITICS, ANARCHY AND REBELLION

At the start of Queen Victoria's reign, very few men and no women at all were entitled to vote. The only people given a political voice were the wealthiest men in the country. However, the fight for suffrage increased over the ensuing decades, and more men were given the vote – although British women would not achieve enfranchisement until well into the twentieth century. As the vote expanded, it necessarily encompassed differing political views, and a more "radical" or socially aware political scene began to take shape. By the end of the nineteenth century, political parties had been forced to look more closely at social necessity and the political platform was beginning to have more relevance for British people of all social classes.

GLADSTONE v. DISRAELI

The two giants of Victorian politics were William Ewart Gladstone and Benjamin Disraeli. Even though she was supposed to be politically neutral, Queen Victoria made it very obvious she favoured Disraeli, a fact that the media was keen to elaborate upon.

BENJAMIN DISRAELI (1804–81)

Born in Bloomsbury, London, Disraeli was the son of an Italian-Jewish writer, Isaac D'Israeli, who gave his children a good private education.

As British society was very anti-Semitic at this time, the family anglicized their name to Disraeli. The children were also baptized in the Anglican Christian religion. Benjamin was 12 years old when he converted from Judaism – although he remained proud of his Jewish heritage and, as an adult and a celebrity, was happy to play up his "exoticism".

As a young man, Disraeli trained as a solicitor, but was never particularly interested in working in the legal system. He was an inveterate risk-taker, and at the age of 20 lost all his money gambling on the stock exchange. Despite this loss, he remained a gambler throughout his life, often struggling through debt, and suffered a nervous breakdown as a result. He had attempted to regain his fortune by becoming a celebrated writer, but when his novel *Vivian Grey* was first published, it was hugely criticized. This exacerbated his depression. Later novels, however, would prove much more popular.

In the 1830s, Disraeli stood as a Whig MP, but was unsuccessful; he decided to become a "progressive Tory" instead. Had his parents not chosen to have their children's faith converted to Anglicanism, Disraeli would not have been allowed to become an MP, as Jews were excluded from Parliament until 1858. In 1837, he was elected to represent Maidstone in Kent. His maiden speech – on the subject of Irish elections – was very poorly received. He ended it with the prophetic words: "Though I sit down now, the time will come when you will hear me."

In 1839, he made an advantageous marriage to a very wealthy widow, Mary Wyndham Lewis. Many critics ridiculed the marriage, as Mary was 12 years older than he, but it was a love match. They had no children, but worked together regularly when she edited his novels. Their relationship was close and adoring, with Mary happy to talk about her feelings for her husband in a manner that was highly unusual for the times. She famously shocked a group of society women by her blunt remark, during a conversation about fair skin, "I wish you could see my Dizzy in his bath!"

In 1841, Disraeli became MP for Shrewsbury, although the prime minister, Robert Peel, overlooked him when he was forming his Parliament. In 1852, Lord Derby appointed Disraeli chancellor of the exchequer. This role only lasted a few months, as the leader of the rival party, William Gladstone, tore Disraeli's budget to political shreds and helped bring down the Tory government.

In 1858, Lord Derby became prime minister again and made Disraeli chancellor and leader of the House of Commons. In 1866, Disraeli was made chancellor again, in the government formed by Lord Derby. When Derby resigned in 1868, Disraeli became prime minister – only to be rapidly replaced at the general election by Gladstone's Liberal party.

Disraeli was a charismatic politician, who became as well known for his flamboyant dress, his romantic demeanour, his sense of adventure and his novels as he was for his political career. In later life, photographs of Disraeli appear to show him wearing a kind of stage make-up, suggesting he was consciously creating a public persona. In 1872, however, he was devastated by the personal tragedy of his wife's death, commenting, "I am totally unable to meet the catastrophe."

Throwing himself into his work to escape his grief, Disraeli was voted in as prime minister again in 1874, at the age of 70. This was the first time since 1841 that the Tories had a clear majority. He worked tirelessly and his reforms included the 1874 Factory Act; the 1875 Public Health Act; the 1875 Artisans' and Labourers' Dwellings Improvement Act (slum clearances and rebuilding); the 1875 Pure Food and Drugs Act; and the 1875 Climbing Boys Act (outlawing child labour for chimney sweeps).

In 1878, he became the first prime minister to attend an international summit: thanks to the growth of the railways, he was able to participate in the Congress of Berlin to discuss the issue of Russia in Turkey. He returned to a hero's welcome and told the crowd he had secured "peace with honour".

DISRAELI THE NOVELIST

As well as a politician, Disraeli was also a popular sensationalist novelist. Several of his books reflect his feelings about the parliamentary system and the state of English poverty, advocating that the rich should help alleviate poverty, not accept it. His novels include: *Vivian Grey* (1826); *The Young Duke* (1831); *Contarini Fleming* (1832); *Alroy* (1833); *Henrietta Temple* (1837); *Venetia* (1837); *Coningsby* (1844); *Sybil, or The Two Nations* (1845); *Tancred* (1847); and *Endymion* (1880).

In 1876, Disraeli had earned even more affection from the Queen by suggesting that she accept the title Empress of India. In 1879, Queen Victoria gave him the title of Lord Beaconsfield. However, the 1879 war with Afghanistan proved to be his political downfall. In 1880, Gladstone became prime minister and Disraeli retired. He died in Mayfair in 1881.

WILLIAM EWART GLADSTONE (1809–98)

Born in Liverpool to Scottish parents, Gladstone was educated at Eton and then Christ Church, Oxford. He intended to be a barrister. At Oxford, he earned a reputation as a great orator and debater, and decided to go into politics. In 1832 he was elected a Tory MP and in 1834–35 he held junior offices in Robert Peel's government. When the Tory party split in 1846, Gladstone followed Peel to become a Liberal-Conservative.

In 1839, Gladstone married Catherine Glynne, with whom he had eight children (four boys and four girls). Catherine helped him greatly in his career and Gladstone wrote to her constantly about his campaigns. In 1859, he changed allegiance again, to the Liberals; after the resignation of Lord Palmerston in 1867, he became leader of the Liberal Party. In 1868, he became prime minister for the first time, an office he held until 1874. In 1877–80, he was rector of the University of Glasgow and in 1880 he became prime minister for the second time. He resigned in 1885, when his government's budget was defeated.

Gladstone was very religious and was also fascinated by ancient Greece. He produced a number of works on these subjects, a stark contrast to Disraeli's sentimental and sensationalist novels. He oversaw the first Education Act of 1870, and he tried to alleviate the plight of prostitutes, working with philanthropists to help save women who had largely been forced into their situation by poverty and desperation. He risked constant slurs on his name and smutty suggestions as to why he was concerning himself with prostitutes. His wife understood his motivations, however, and refused to let him bow to pressure.

In 1885, Gladstone was offered an earldom by Queen Victoria, but he declined because he preferred to stay in office. As the Queen was not a fan of his, the offer of an earldom was widely believed to have been prompted by her desire to remove him from Parliament. The following year, he became prime minister for the third time. His first bill on home rule for Ireland split the Liberal party and was rejected. For years, the spectre of the Irish home rule issue was to haunt Gladstone's career as he sought to give the Irish more autonomy over their government and was constantly criticized for doing so. Despite the controversy of his home rule beliefs, he remained a popular politician, and in 1892 he became prime minister for the fourth time (until 1894).

Gladstone's last public speech was in Liverpool, the place of his birth, in 1896, by which time he was already suffering from the cancer that killed him. He spoke against the atrocities that were being carried out in Turkey, where Armenians had been massacred for being Christians. After Gladstone's death in May 1898, the University of Glasgow erected a bronze statue of him in George Square. It was paid for by public subscription.

THE POOR LAWS

There had been Poor Laws in Britain for centuries, but during the nineteenth century these gradually began to be reformed. In 1834, the Act for the Amendment and Better Administration of the Laws Relating to the Poor in England and Wales was passed. It replaced many laws that had been in force for hundreds of years and set up a more cohesive central system – which relied heavily on the creation of more workhouses. When Queen Victoria came to the throne, workhouses and the new Poor Law were fully in effect. Letters to newspaper editors at the time show that many people were appalled by the way the country's poorest were being treated. In 1843, an article in *The Morning Post* (the newspaper that had published an unknown writer named Charles Dickens a few years earlier) railed against the Poor Law and the pious belief that it was working to reduce levels of poverty:

> *It is self-evident, moreover, that if we accompany the relief which we bestow with pain and sorrow, and give the starving the bread of bitterness to eat, men will submit to much privation before they accept the proffered assistance; and to congratulate ourselves upon the decrease of pauperism is as absurd as Louis the Fourteen, after his dragonades, and the revocation of the edict of Nantes, to express his gratification at the number of Protestant converts.*

In 1834, Edwin Chadwick published a report on the Poor Laws; his findings caused a new Poor Law Commission to be set up, of which he was made secretary. Chadwick worked tirelessly to try and bring his findings to the people who made the laws, but most politicians were reluctant to make the kind of changes that he knew were needed.

Following deadly outbreaks of typhoid in Britain in 1837–38, Chadwick finally began to be listened to. In 1842, he and Dr Thomas Southwood Smith produced their crucial report, "The Sanitary Conditions of the Labouring Population of Great Britain". This highlighted the link between poor health and insanitary living conditions. The Poor Law Commission did not want to be associated with the report, as they knew MPs would not welcome its recommendations, so Chadwick paid for its publication. It was a crucial document which pointed out the astonishing failures in public healthcare and the terrible conditions in which so many people in Britain, particularly in the most crowded areas of big cities, lived – making a direct correlation between poor housing and poor health.

Despite the horrified reactions of MPs in the House of Commons to the report and the widespread reporting of Chadwick's and Southwood Smith's findings in the media, the Conservative government chose to reject the findings. The recommendations made were far too costly for the government to want to act on them. It was not until a Liberal government – under prime minister Lord John Russell – took power in 1847 that the report was finally acted upon. It led to the passing of a new Public Health Act in 1848, just after another outbreak of deadly disease (this time it was cholera).

The Act introduced many new healthcare policies and a central health board. It also started to make local councils and other local organizations take responsibility for the health and wellbeing of their residents – for example, in areas where the death rate was particularly high, local health boards needed to be set up.

Amongst the recommendations that Chadwick and Southwood Smith had suggested were:
- The providing of clean drinking water.
- The regular removal of rubbish from roads and residences.
- Improved drainage.
- The creation of more modern and effective sewers.
- The appointment of a medical officer for every town.

THE ANTI-SLAVERY MOVEMENT

The year after Queen Victoria came to the throne saw the final abolition of slavery in British colonies. It had taken many years and successful public protests, such as the eighteenth-century boycotts of slave-produced sugar and rum, but at last nineteenth-century Britain had caught up with its eighteenth-century ideology.

A TIMELINE OF BRITISH SLAVERY

- 1660s – Britain becomes a slave-trading and slave-owning nation.
- 1791 – Parliament rejects the Abolition of Slavery bill.
- 1792 – The public boycott of slave-grown sugar and sugar products (such as rum) from the West Indies begins; people either manage without or buy sugar imported from the East Indies, where the workers are not enslaved.
- 25 March 1807 – The Abolition of the Slave Trade Act is passed. Although slave ships are no longer permitted to trade in the British Isles, protestors are angry that nothing is being done to help or free slaves elsewhere in the British Empire.
- 1816 – Slaves rebel in Barbados. It becomes known as "the Easter Rebellion".
- 1820s – The sugar boycott is revived as British abolitionists push forward once again for the abolition of slavery in all British colonies and protectorates.
- 1823 – Abolitionist groups from around the country come together to form the Anti-Slavery Society. Within a year, there are more than 200 branches of the society throughout Britain.
- 1823 – A slave rebellion takes place in Demerara, British Guyana, a sugar-producing area – the slaves have heard that slavery is no longer legal in Britain. The rebellion is led by Jack Gladstone.
- 1828 – Mary Prince, a slave from Bermuda, arrives in London with the family who "own" her. She escapes from her employers. The Abolition Society helps her publish *The History of Mary Prince, a West Indian Slave. Related by Herself*. Between now and 1833, the government is inundated by petitions signed by more than 1.5 million Britons calling for the end of slavery.
- 1831–32 – The Christmas Rebellion in Jamaica is led by Sam Sharpe.

- 29 August 1833 – The Emancipation of Slaves Act is passed. This grants freedom to all slaves within the British Empire, although a time stricture is imposed; in some cases this means up to six more years of slavery. Plantation owners are compensated richly for the loss of their slaves.
- 1 August 1834 – The Emancipation of Slaves Act comes into force. Many plantation owners in the West Indies still refuse to honour the law.
- 1 August 1838 – All slaves are finally freed in all British territories, including the West Indies.

Oh the horrors of slavery! – How the thought of it pains my heart! But the truth ought to be told of it; and what my eyes have seen I think it is my duty to relate; for few people in England know what slavery is. I have been a slave – I have felt what a slave feels, and I know what a slave knows; and I would have all the good people in England to know it too, that they may break our chains, and set us free.

From *The History of Mary Prince, a West Indian Slave.*
Related by Herself, 1831

In 1837 it was estimated that 80 per cent of the British population lived in the countryside. By the 1850s, more than 50 per cent of the population was living in a town or city.

THE CORN LAWS

For the first nine years of Queen Victoria's reign, a hotly debated topic – from within the Houses of Parliament to working men's pubs – was the Corn Laws. This was an issue that had been raging since the time of King George III.

- In 1791, war overseas caused financial problems in Britain and the resultant legislation led to rising grain prices.
- In 1795, a poor harvest led to a scarcity of grain (an essential food staple of the British diet) and food riots.

- More years of bad harvests led to increasing poverty in agricultural communities and tension between the workers, the farmers and the government.
- In 1815, Britain had just come to the end of war with France and was desperate for revenue. An Act of Parliament was passed that refused importation of any foreign corn, until the price of British-grown corn had been elevated to a higher price.
- This new Corn Law led to more resentment between the agricultural industry and the politicians in Westminster, but more importantly it raised the price of a necessary food far beyond the purses of the working classes.
- Over the next few years, farmers became increasingly worried and, as a result, began reducing their workforces.
- In 1828, the government – under the Duke of Wellington – revised the Corn Law again. Wellington's new measures did little to alleviate the problems of the poor or of the struggling agricultural industry.
- In 1836, an Anti-Corn-Law Association was founded in London, but made little progress.
- In 1838, the year after Queen Victoria came to the throne, a new group was founded in Manchester. This was much better organized and it was named the Anti-Corn-Law League (ACLL) in 1839.
- The ACLL was much more effective than any previous campaigns had been and people around the country began to discuss and take notice of what had been happening to the farm workers.
- In 1846, the prime minister, Robert Peel, repealed the Corn Laws.

THE GREAT STINK

During the long hot summer of 1858, the expression "Parliament stinks" would have been very accurate. London, the seat of the British Parliament, was sweltering in a heat wave and enduring the constant stench of rotting matter rising up from the River Thames. Those London residents who were able to do so fled the city.

The problem was caused by the years and years of using the river as a rubbish dump and sewer, in the ignorant belief that the water could cope with everything thrown into it. The "Great Stink", as it became known, was so bad that businesses, including several courts of justice, were forced to close. Initially Parliament attempted to keep going, hanging sheets soaked in lime chloride across all the windows in an effort to mask the smell. However, when that proved ineffective against the river than ran (or, rather, stagnated) just outside the House of Commons and House of Lords, Parliament also closed.

In an article entitled "The State of the Thames" that month, *The Examiner* newspaper reported:

> *The administration of justice runs the risk of being suspended at Westminster in consequence of the foul condition at low water of stinking Father Thames. – In the Court of Queen's Bench, on Wednesday, Mr James called the attention of Lord Campbell to the foul state of the court and passages.... Mr J. Bredall, a surgeon, who was attending the Court as a witness in the cause which was being tried, here came forward, and, being sworn, said he had been compelled to leave the Court three times in consequence of the bad smells. The atmosphere in Court became irrespirable, and it was quite as bad in the passages. The smells came from the Thames, or from sewage of some kind. He gave it as his opinion, as a medical man, that it was dangerous to breathe this atmosphere. He thought it would be dangerous to the lives of the jurymen, counsel, and witnesses to remain. It would produce malaria, and perhaps typhus fever.*
>
> **The Examiner, 26 June 1858**

For years, sanitary engineers and campaigners had been attempting to make the government aware of the desperate need for a new system of sewers beneath London. In the summer of the Great Stink, it took MPs just 18 days to make the decision to build them.

It wasn't only London that had problems with archaic and ineffective sewers, and once the newspapers had reported on the Great Stink they began to turn their attention to other parts of the country. A new breed of innovative engineers had been born and they were desperate to be able to put their new skills to use. Throughout the rest of Queen Victoria's reign, Britain's drainage and sewage systems were extensively overhauled. In the summer of 1889, a Local Board of

Health meeting was held in Cambridge and published the following minutes:

The Drains
The Board proceeded to consider the question of the drains ... there ought to be systematical flushing of the sewers, the stench on Sunday last being simply abominable. The Board ... directed the surveyor (Mr Kemp) to properly attend to the matter, and do what was required for the sanitary condition of the drains.

Water Closets
Mr Tandy called attention to the nuisances arising in certain parts of the town from the bad and filthy condition of the water-closets. It was decided to serve notice upon the owners, and if the closets were not properly cleaned out in due time the Board would do the work and charge the owners with it.

The Water Supply
A letter from the Local Government Board was read, asking what steps the Board had decided to take with reference to the polluted shallow wells from which the water of the town was derived. The clerk of the Board was directed to reply, stating the matter was receiving their earnest consideration.

JOSEPH BAZALGETTE (1819–91)

The man chosen to build the new sewers was the engineer Joseph Bazalgette. He had been born into a naval family but, after showing an interest in engineering, was apprenticed to Sir John McNeill (who, in turn, had been a student of the eighteenth-century engineer Thomas Telford). In 1842, Bazalgette set up his own engineering practice and within a few years had been commissioned to look at the issue of London's sewage problem. In 1856, he was made chief engineer at the newly created Metropolitan Board of Works in London, and set about creating a new sanitary scheme for the overcrowded and disease-ridden city. His work would go on to influence public sanitation and public-health projects around the world. In *The Observer* newspaper, Bazalgette's plans were described as "the most extensive and wonderful work of modern times" (14 April 1861). Bazalgette was knighted by Queen Victoria in 1874.

THE FIGHT FOR EQUALITY

The year after Queen Victoria came to power, the political reformers known as Chartists drew up their People's Charter. Ten years later, tens of thousands of workers marched from all over the country to London to deliver a petition asking for equal rights for workers and all social classes. In the People's Charter of 1838, a clause about women's suffrage was included; however, it was removed in revised editions. The Victorian era saw – ironically, given the sovereign was female – a step backwards for the women's movement. In the eighteenth century, the fight for equality had seemed to be drawing closer, but by the mid-nineteenth century it was firmly off the political agenda.

THE VICTORIAN WIFE

In 1854, the poet Coventry Patmore published "The Angel in the House", a long poem about how the perfect wife put her husband's happiness before all else. No matter how badly a man behaved, a true Victorian wife would always forgive him. The poem provided the model for the "perfect Victorian woman": selfless, pious, chaste and submissive.

In 1855, the social campaigner Caroline Norton – who had escaped her abusive marriage but had her children taken away from her by her bullying husband – sent a 30,000-word pamphlet to Queen Victoria about the gross inequalities that existed between the rights of men and women in marriage. It had taken her two decades of campaigning, but her work would help bring about political changes, initially in the wording of the 1857 Marriage and Divorce Act.

The Queen was not usually supportive of women's concerns and was fervently against female suffrage. When she discovered that Lady Amberley, one of the women in her court, had been made president of her local suffrage society, she wrote in a private letter that Lady Amberley ought to be "whipped" for such an outrage.

One of the most important men to support female suffrage was the lawyer Dr Richard Pankhurst (later husband of Emmeline and father of Christabel and Sylvia). He sought to have female suffrage recognized as part of the 1867 Reform Act (his proposal was rejected, and it would take until 1928 for full female suffrage to be granted in Britain). In 1870, he drew up the highly influential Married Women's Property Act, the first step on the very long road to equality in marriage.

Other important campaigners included Josephine Butler, who fought against the sexual abuse sanctioned in the Contagious Diseases Acts; Frances Power Cobbe, who fought for sexual equality as well as for the rights of animals (she founded the first National Anti-Vivisection Society); and Millicent Garrett Fawcett, sister of Elizabeth Garrett Anderson and president of the National Union of Women's Suffrage Societies (NUWSS).

9

POVERTY AND PHILANTHROPY

Queen Victoria reigned over a country blighted by poverty. Nineteenth-century Britain was a place where the rich were excessively rich and the poor were often starving. Throughout the Queen's reign, there was a huge growth in philanthropic movements, and by the end of the Victorian age many people were far better off than they had been at the start – although this was due almost entirely to the efforts of social campaigners and charities rather than to the actions of politicians. The Victorian age was a time of social campaigning, and witnessed the founding of many important charitable movements and societies.

THE IRISH POTATO FAMINE

Between 1846 and 1851, more than a million people died in Ireland as a consequence of the potato crops failing and the subsequent ineptitude by Queen Victoria's governments to deal effectively with the problem (not least because politicians accused the Irish of overstating the problem). The potato famine, also known as "the Great Hunger", was particularly brutal because the people of Ireland had become so dependent on potato crops and, as a result, grew almost nothing else. When the potatoes were attacked by blight the Irish had no other food crops to fall back on.

Even before the famine, the plight of most people in Ireland was a truly terrible one. Huge swathes of the Irish countryside had been bought by wealthy Irish and English people – these were mostly absentee landlords, not interested in the welfare of their workers nor in the condition of their homes. Most people lived in abject poverty, with whole families crowded into one insanitary room.

The Whig prime minister Lord John Russell was particularly despised for his lack of compassion; his belief was that Ireland's wealthy should help the Irish poor and he refused to send English aid. Eventually, in 1847 – by which time thousands of people had died – he sent a small amount of relief, but when that didn't prove enough and angry people started protesting, he sent in troops and declared martial law. In addition to the failure of the crops, there were outbreaks of cholera, typhoid and dysentery.

In 1841 the Irish census set the country's population at 8.2 million. The census of 1851 recorded a population of 6.5 million.

PAINTINGS OF POVERTY

The artist George Frederic Watts painted many socially conscious pictures, such as *Found Drowned*, which shows a young female suicide, the victim of the cruelty and misogyny of the Victorian legal and social system. In *c.*1848–50 he painted *The Irish Famine*, which depicts a young and desperate Irish family who have been made homeless and destitute. The painting was a cry from the heart, a visual depiction of starvation, as the emaciated parents and listless children seem to waste away before the very eyes of the viewer. The father looks out blankly as though stunned, but his fists are clenched in impotent fury at his inability to feed his family.

Slowly, gradually, and with a voice that was for a long time discredited, the news spread itself through the country that the food of the people was gone. That his own crop was rotten and useless each cotter quickly knew, and realized the idea that he must work for wages if he could get them, or else go to the poorhouse. That the crop of his parish or district was gone became evident to the priest, and the parson, and the squire; and they realized the idea that they must fall on other parishes or other districts for support. But it was long

*before the fact made itself known that there was no food in
any parish, in any district.*

From *Castle Richmond* by Anthony Trollope, 1861

THE SCOTTISH POTATO FAMINE

In 1846, the potato blight arrived in Scotland and left devastation in its
wake. As in Ireland, it was the poorest people who suffered most. The
blight had made it to Ireland and then to Scotland from North America,
and continued to damage Scottish crops until the late 1850s.

THE HIGHLAND CLEARANCES

Towards the end of the eighteenth century, farming in the Scottish
Highlands had begun to undergo a dramatic change: the landowners
switched from arable farming to sheep farming. Arable farming had
needed huge armies of workers, all of whom were housed on the
land. When the farmers began raising sheep, they needed far fewer
workers – and they began turning their former labourers out of their
homes.

The clearances began in the 1780s, and within a decade the first mass
migration of people had begun. 1792 became known as "the year of
the sheep" – so many people were cleared off the land to make way for
animals that a massive percentage of the population ended up on ships
to Canada, New Zealand and Australia.

WORKHOUSES

Three years before Queen Victoria came to the throne, the Poor Law
Amendment Act of 1834 had been passed. This stated that no "able-
bodied person" could claim any kind of poor relief unless they were
living in a poorhouse, also known as a workhouse. As the name suggests,
these were not refuges, but places where people worked – and worked
very long hours performing menial and painful tasks – in order to have
a roof over their heads, and to be provided with clothes (a humiliating
uniform) and a very meagre diet.

Within a few years, the word "workhouse" had come to be associated with fear and cruelty. If a couple or a family had no choice but to enter the workhouse, they knew they would be split up, as there were separate wards for men, women and children, and no facilities to accommodate families. If relatives or friends tried to communicate with, or see, each other they were punished. Discipline was strictly enforced and offenders were punished by being placed in solitary confinement, being put on "short rations" (receiving less food than other inmates) or with beatings. The workhouse was the very last resort, and many people preferred to starve on the streets rather than end up in one.

DR BARNARDO (1845–05)

Born in Dublin in 1845, Thomas John Barnardo was 16 when he converted from Catholicism to evangelical Protestantism, a hugely controversial move in Ireland. In 1866, he moved to London and began training as a doctor at the London Hospital in Whitechapel. His intention was to work in China as a medical missionary.

Within a few months of Barnardo's arrival in London, there was an outbreak of cholera; it raged through the East End, devastating the communities where he was training. The infection claimed thousands of victims and hundreds of children were orphaned. As Barnardo walked to and from work, he became aware of even more children than usual sleeping rough, begging and lying ill on the streets – they had no parents left to help them and no homes to go to.

Barnardo was determined to do something to help these children, and in 1867 he set up a school for poor children. As he had no idea where most of the children lived, one of the boys, a child named Jim Jarvis, agreed to take Barnardo on a tour of the East End. Barnardo recorded seeing children sleeping inside gutters and on rooftops. This determined him to change their lives.

In 1870, the very first Barnardo Home for Boys opened in Stepney, in East London. The children were not only housed, but they were also trained in essential skills, including carpentry, metalwork and cobbling – all of which would help them find jobs. Wanting to ensure the home was free from the problems caused by overcrowding, Barnardo limited the numbers of children who could spend the night there. On one night, this policy meant that a boy was turned away; when this same child was found dead on the street a couple of days later, Barnardo blamed himself. From that time onwards, his policy was to accept any destitute child.

In 1873, Barnardo married a fellow social campaigner, Syrie Elmslie. Together they founded their first home for girls. The Barnardos helped thousands of children. When Thomas Barnardo died in 1905, there were almost 100 Barnardos homes caring for over 8,000 children. His work continues today in the charity that bears his name.

GEORGE PEABODY (1795–1869)

In 1837, George Peabody from Massachussetts, USA, arrived in Britain. He was a merchant banker looking to make his fortune – and he also changed the face of what is now known as social housing.

Some years after setting up in investment banking as George Peabody & Co., Peabody began to look for a business partner. He met a man almost 20 years his junior, Junius Spencer Morgan, and together they set up a company called Peabody, Morgan & Co (many years later it would become known as Morgan Grenfell).

In the 1860s, Peabody set up the Peabody Trust to help provide housing for people who could not afford the high London rents. The population of London was growing all the time, so landlords could always find tenants for their buildings, no matter what state they were in. In addition, the building of the railways had forced many people out of their homes when land had been compulsorily purchased by the railway companies, and overcrowding was a major issue in the poorest areas.

Peabody died in 1869, by which time he had become lauded as a hero. He was given a temporary burial in Westminster Abbey, before his body was repatriated back to the USA.

Be friendly with selected people but not intimate with anyone.

George Peabody's advice to his nephew

ANGELA BURDETT-COUTTS (1814–1906)

The young Angela Burdett never expected to become the richest woman in England, but her grandfather, the banking millionaire Thomas Coutts, made her his heiress. He made an intelligent choice, as Angela (who added the Coutts name to her surname in honour of her grandfather) was a true Victorian philanthropist and made good use of his money after he died. She worked on schemes to help women, children, animals and anyone in need. She was an education and healthcare reformer, and worked closely with Charles Dickens on a number of projects until she became angered by Dickens's decision to separate from his wife Catherine in 1858 – their friendship never recovered.

OCTAVIA HILL (1838–1912)

Born into a comfortable middle-class home, Octavia Hill's father, James Hill, fought against corruption and cruelty, while her mother, Caroline Hill, set up a school for local children and became an education reformer. When her father became bankrupt, the family was forced to live in very different circumstances and James suffered a mental breakdown; Caroline took on responsibility for the family. Together, James and Caroline Hill set in motion their daughter's future as a social reformer. Octavia dedicated her life to housing reform: she funded and helped to set up housing schemes for the poor, wrote articles about the injustices suffered by the people she was helping, and helped to create the Kyrle Society ("to bring beauty home to the people") together with her sister Miranda (an enterprise supported by William Morris). She was a staunch campaigner of preserving the countryside and was also a co-founder of the National Trust.

HENRY MAYHEW (1812–87)

In 1851, the journalist and social reformer Henry Mayhew published his seminal work *London Labour and the London Poor*. Until this time, Mayhew had been known as a radical journalist and as the co-founder of the satirical magazine *Punch* (which was first published in 1841). With this work, he became recognized as an investigative reporter and social scientist. The book was made up of a series of interviews and articles, inspired by his days spent walking the poorest streets of the city and recording the conversations he had with everyone he met: child labourers, sewage workers, prostitutes, street sweepers, costermongers, shopkeepers, market traders, seamstresses, the homeless, the destitute and those considered insane and helpless. He was giving a voice to those people who had never had a chance to have their say before. The book caused a sensation.

LONDON LABOUR AND THE LONDON POOR

- *"It's awful to see some poor women, too, trying to pick up a living in the streets by selling nuts or oranges. It's awful to see them, for they can't set about it right; besides that, there's too many before they start. They don't find a living, it's only another way of starving."* (From an interview with a costermonger)
- *"Why, sir,"* said one man ... *"I myself have slept in the top room of a house nor far from Drury-lane, and you could study the stars, if you were so minded, through the holes left by the slates having been blown off the roof."* The same man told me ... that he had scraped together a handful of bugs from the bed-clothes, and crushed them under a candlestick, and had done that many a time ... He had slept in rooms so crammed with sleepers – he believed there were 30 where 12 would have been a proper number – that their breaths in the dead of night and in the unventilated chamber rose (I use his own words) *"in one foul, choking steam of stench"*.
- *"I dare say there ain't ten out of a hundred girls what's living with men, what's been married Church of England fashion."* (From an interview with a coster-girl)
- *The rat-catcher's dress is usually a velveteen jacket, strong corduroy trousers, and laced boots. Round his shoulder he wears an oil-skin belt, on which are painted the figures of huge rats, with fierce-looking eyes and formidable whiskers.... Occasionally – and in the country far more than in town – he carries in his hand an iron cage in which are ferrets, while two or three crop-eared terriers dog his footsteps. Sometimes a tamed rat runs about his shoulder and arms, or nestles in his bosom or in the large pockets of his coat.*

- *These poor creatures are certainly about the most deplorable in their appearance of any I have met with in the course of my inquiries…. It cannot be said that they are clad in rags, for they are scarcely half covered by the tattered indescribable things that serve them for clothing; their bodies are grimed with the foul soil of the river, and their torn garments stiffened up like boards with dirt of every possible description. Among the mud-larks may be seen many old women, and it is indeed pitiable to behold them, especially during the winter, bent nearly double with age and infirmity, paddling and groping among the wet mud for small pieces of coal, chips of wood, or any sort of refuse washed up by the tide.* (Mud-larks were usually children who spent their lives searching through the stinking river mud in the hopes of finding something useful or valuable.)

A picture of human life so wonderful, so awful … so exciting and terrible.

William Thackeray about *London Labour and the London Poor*

INVESTIGATIVE JOURNALISM

"Society … outwardly, indeed, appears white and glistening, but within is full of dead men's bones and rottenness." So said the investigative journalist W. T. Stead, who in July 1885 undertook his most controversial project to date. On 4 July, he warned his readers to prepare themselves for a story that would "open the eyes of the public". He had been aware for some years of a campaign that was constantly ignored by those in power and he was determined to bring it to the forefront of the public's consciousness.

Stead was on a mission to expose a particularly sickening Victorian social ill – that London had become the European centre of child sex trafficking. He wanted to prove partly to his readers and particularly to the government how prevalent the trade was in selling children for sex. What Stead wanted his articles to do was to bring about a change in the law, not least because the current "age of consent" was 13 years old. He wanted the lawmakers to stop ignoring the problem and to start working to protect Britain's children, as well as the children who were trafficked to Britain from overseas.

Stead spent several nights undercover in the East End of London so that he could prove how easy it was to "buy" the services of a young girl for just £5 and to expose those who preyed on the children. In his four-part article "The Maiden Tribute of Modern Babylon", which was published in *The Pall Mall Gazette* – of which he was editor – he revealed the extent of the sex trade. The articles were published daily, on 6, 7, 8 and 10 July 1885, and named many of the perpetrators as well as the corrupt doctors who were willing to "guarantee" a child's virginity to prospective clients.

Stead's article, as promised, shocked his readers. He wrote heartbreakingly of raped children "snared, trapped and outraged, either when under the influence of drugs or after a prolonged struggle in a locked room". He wrote of the "gloating" rich men who abused working-class "daughters". The effect was immediate. In August 1885, "An Act to Make Further Provision for the Protection of Women and Girls and the Suppression of Brothels and Other Purposes" was passed. This included raising the age of heterosexual sexual consent to 16.

One repercussion of the article was that Stead was made a scapegoat for his uncovering of the trade in children. For the purposes of his article he had paid £5 to "buy" a girl named Eliza Armstrong (in his articles he changed her name to Lily). As a result, he was prosecuted under the new Act and sentenced to three months in prison.

> *London's lust annually uses up many thousands of women, who are literally killed and made away with – living sacrifices slain in the service of vice.*
> **W. T. Stead, "The Maiden Tribute of Modern Babylon I: the Report of our Secret Commission", *The Pall Mall Gazette*, 6 July 1885**

MODEL VILLAGES

William Hesketh Lever (1851–1925) grew up in middle-class comfort in Bolton, Lancashire. He began his career in his father's grocery business and ended up in partnership with his younger brother, James, creating the company Lever Brothers. In 1886, they launched their first significant new creation, Sunlight Soap. This was remarkable for using only plant-derived ingredients, instead of the smelly animal tallow usually found in soap. Sunlight Soap made the Lever brothers' fortunes.

Within a couple of years, William had begun to put his philanthropic principles into practice and decided to build a model village for his workers to live in. This was in addition to paying his workers much fairer wages than most factory workers could expect, and crucial benefits packets for workers and their families. The idealized community he created was named after the product that had made him rich: Port Sunlight.

> *Sweating the machine and not the worker makes possible and profitable the six-hour day... It should not be inferred that the six-hour day means working the plant only six hours. The idea is to work the plant double time – twelve hours – with the two six hour shifts.*
>
> **William Hesketh Lever**

Lever commissioned 30 architects to create his idealized English village, with buildings based on styles from Shakespeare's time. Port Sunlight took several decades to complete, with work beginning in 1888 and only coming to a halt in 1914 with the outbreak of war. The workers were given the unusual luxuries of indoor lavatories and bathrooms in all of the homes, a school for the children, training classes for women and older girls, a library, a gym, a concert hall, a theatre and even an open-air swimming pool. All of this cost one-fifth of a worker's pay. In return for such easy living conditions, Lever expected a very high standard of behaviour from his workers. Anyone who broke any of the strict rules that governed life in Port Sunlight was asked to leave.

In addition to treating his own workers fairly, Lever tried to influence working practices across Britain. He had shown by example that it was possible to become a millionaire without exploiting one's workers, and he tried to ensure that others did likewise. He led campaigns for a shorter working day.

☙ In the early twentieth century, William Hesketh Lever became known as Lord Leverhulme, because "Hulme" was his wife's maiden name. He was a passionate art collector, and later created and dedicated an art gallery to his wife – the Lady Lever Art Gallery at Port Sunlight.

☙ **Lord Leverhulme Overseas**
Although Lord Leverhulme was renowned for the fairness with which he treated his workers in Britain, sadly his principles did not extend overseas. In the early twentieth century, he sourced palm oil from Africa, and bought it from a plantation in what was then known as the Belgian Congo, where the workers were treated almost like slaves and paid very poor wages. It was a far cry from the haven Leverhulme had created in Port Sunlight.

OTHER MODEL VILLAGES

- In the late 1840s, Great Western Railway turned the small market town of Swindon into a railway town, with housing built for its workers. By 1850 it was ready to be a community, complete with a free health service.
- In 1851, the textile manufacturer Titus Salt created the model village of Saltaire in Bradford, West Yorkshire, for his workers.
- Price's Village near Liverpool was created in 1854 for the workers at the Price's Candle Factory. It was said to have inspired William Lever to build Port Sunlight.
- Hartley's Village in Aintree was founded in 1886 for the workers at the Hartley's Jam factory.
- Creswell's Model Village in Derbyshire was completed in 1895 for the workers at the Bolsover Colliery Company.

GEORGE CADBURY (1839–1922)

Another philanthropic manufacturer was George Cadbury, who built the Bourneville model village alongside the chocolate factory. Bourneville, not far from Birmingham, was intended to "alleviate the evils of modern more cramped living conditions", as Cadbury explained. The first houses were built in the 1880s for senior employees, as the factory was being built. Over the next decade, Cadbury worked with architects on plans for a village with green spaces, where every worker's home could have its own garden. This was a far cry from the pollution of nearby Birmingham, where most of his workers were currently living. By the mid-1890s, over 140 workers' cottages had been built and the grounds were landscaped to ensure that there were parks for the workers to use, as well as their gardens. Cadbury also set up a medical centre, sporting facilities and pension plans, and he encouraged workers' committees.

10

THE BRITISH EMPIRE

When Queen Victoria inherited the British throne, she also inherited an enormous overseas empire. In the time of her grandfather King George III, the empire had lost its American "colony", but under Victoria's reign it continued to expand, most notably into Asia and Africa. The huge swathes of the world over which the Queen was claimed to preside were so vast that the empire became known as that "on which the sun never sets".

EMPRESS OF INDIA

In 1877, the British public learnt that the Queen had a new title. The prime minister, Benjamin Disraeli, had suggested that she become known as the Empress of India. It had been a controversial subject for over a year, hotly debated in Parliament and the royal household, but Disraeli and the Queen won through. Many people believed that the Queen's desire to become an empress had been prompted by the marriages of her children. Her eldest daughter, Vicky, would become Empress of Prussia and, in 1874, Prince Alfred had married the Grand Duchess Marie of Russia – she was a great lover of grandeur, and it was claimed she had made comments about a tsar and tsarina being more important than a queen. Queen Victoria was not prepared to have her position as most revered person at a royal dinner party, or indeed in the country, usurped.

THE BRITISH EAST INDIA COMPANY
AND THE OPIUM WARS

By the time Queen Victoria came to the throne, the British East India Company had been in operation for over 200 years, trading mainly with China and India. The company imported goods from Asia, including spices, tea, porcelain, silks, cottons and drugs (in particular opium). It also exported British products to its trading partners, the most coveted of which – in China – was silver.

By the nineteenth century, there was an increasing awareness of the scarcity of British silver to be bartered with China. In an attempt to sell the Chinese another coveted commodity instead, the British East India Company traders began to take opium from India to China. Initially this precious commodity – a very powerful medicinal drug – was welcomed, but within a few decades it became obvious that China was suffering. Opium was extremely addictive and the number of Chinese people now struggling with addiction had reached epidemic proportions. The British had been fully aware of the often-fatal effects of opium, but had knowingly traded it with China as a wonderful medicinal drug and sleeping aid.

By the 1830s, it was not only the British East India Company that was supplying China with opium. In 1834 the company had lost its previous monopoly on trading with Asia, and other entrepreneurial European traders had begun to start investing in opium. By this time, the majority of the British East India Company's trade was with India, not China, but when the Chinese authorities threatened to use force against the opium ships, the British East India Company defended the traders' right to free trade and the first Opium War began. It lasted from 1839 until 1842. In 1856–60, France allied with Britain in the second Opium War. The wars cast a long shadow over Chinese history, as they ended with a humiliating defeat at the hands of the European ships and loss of the island of Hong Kong to Britain. As a measure of how little Queen Victoria understood about these international policies, she wrote to King Leopold of Belgium in 1841, "Albert is so amused at my having got the island of Hong Kong."

THE CRIMEAN WAR (1854–56)

Throughout the 1840s, tension built around France, Russia and Britain's competition for influence in the Middle East. Turkey was the access route from Europe to the Middle East and was also where the perceived eastern religion of Islam met the western religion of Christianity – often causing conflict. The once all-powerful Ottoman Empire had started to wane and Tsar Nicholas of Russia saw a chance to expand his own empire. For once Britain and France were united, in their fear of Russian expansion.

On 2 July 1853, the Russia army marched into Romania and began its attack on the Ottoman (Turkish) army. In October, Turkey declared war on Russia. In March 1854, France and Britain declared war on Russia and the Crimean War began. It is chiefly remembered today for its military "blunders" (including the senseless Charge of the Light Brigade), for the pioneering nursing work of Florence Nightingale and Mary Seacole, for the prefabricated war hospital designed by Isambard Kingdom Brunel, and for the great chef Alexis Soyer's invention of the Soyer field stove.

> *Half a league, half a league,*
> *Half a league onward,*
> *All in the valley of Death*
> * Rode the six hundred:*
> *"Forward, the Light Brigade!*
> *Charge for the guns!" he said.*
> *Into the valley of Death*
> * Rode the six hundred.*
>
> *"Forward, the Light Brigade!"*
> *Was there a man dismayed?*
> *Not though the soldier knew*
> * Someone had blundered.*
> * Theirs not to make reply*
> * Theirs not to reason why,*
> * Theirs but to do and die.*
> * Into the valley of Death*
> * Rode the six hundred.*

From "The Charge of the Light Brigade" by Alfred, Lord Tennyson, 1854

☙ *He saved as many lives through his kitchens as Florence Nightingale did through her wards.*

From *The Morning Chronicle's* obituary of Alexis Soyer, 1856

ALEXIS SOYER (1810–56)

Renowned chef Soyer had already witnessed hardship in the 1840s, when he was sent out to Ireland to help combat the 1847 potato famine. There he had set up his revolutionary "soup kitchens" in an attempt to prevent the widespread starvation of the Irish people. In 1855, he headed out to the Crimean battlefields, taking with him his "field stove", which was a portable and economical means of heating food and producing proper meals. One hundred and twenty years after the Crimean War, the British army was still using Soyer's field stove. He also invented the "Scutari teapot" which enabled the making of a satisfying cup of tea with only half the usual amount of tea-leaves. He developed a new type of bread too – known as "biscuit bread" – as it was impossible to get fresh bread, or the correct ingredients to make it, in Scutari. Soyer stayed in the Crimea, providing nourishing meals to British troops, until the end of the war.

CRIMEAN JOURNALISM

The Irish journalist William Howard Russell (1820–1907) made his name in the Crimean War. He was working for *The Times* and sending his eyewitness reports back to London from the Crimea. The stories Russell sent back from the front line changed the way that people viewed the military and ushered in a new era of war reporting: "The commonest accessories of a hospital are wanting ... there is not the least attention paid to decency or cleanliness.... For all I can observe, these men die without the least effort being made to save them.... The sick appear to be tended by the sick, and the dying by the dying."

Russell's work inspired Florence Nightingale, and his report from Balaclava informed one of the most famous poems, "The Charge of the Light Brigade", by Alfred, Lord Tennyson. Russell wrote: "They swept proudly past, glittering in the morning sun in all the pride and splendour of war. We could scarcely believe the evidence of our senses! Surely that handful of men were not going to charge an army in position? Alas, it was but too true – their desperate valour knew no bounds, and far indeed was it removed from its so-called better part – discretion."

FLORENCE NIGHTINGALE (1820–1910)

Born into a wealthy family, Florence Nightingale was named after the Italian city in which she was conceived. She grew up in luxury on a privileged estate in Hampshire – but she felt stifled. In 1852, Nightingale completed an essay entitled "Cassandra" (which Virginia Woolf would later describe as being akin to the author having "shrieked aloud in agony"). The essay deals with the plight of women and reveals Nightingale's fury with what she perceived as the stifling, imprisoning Victorian family. Nightingale's essay is intelligent and angry: "Why…" she wrote, "… have women passion, intellect, moral activity – these three – and a place in society where no one of the three can be exercised?... in the conventional society, which men have made for women, and women have accepted … [women] *must* act the farce of hypocrisy, the lie that they are without passion – and therefore what else can they say to their daughters, without giving the lie to themselves?"

Some years earlier, Florence Nightingale had told her family that she had received a religious calling telling her she should become a nurse. Her wealthy parents were appalled that not only was she intending to have a career, but that she wanted to work in a degrading profession that would require her to have an in-depth knowledge of the male, as well as female, anatomy. Despite fierce opposition, Nightingale remained resolute and trained as a nurse. By the time of writing "Cassandra" she was 32 years old and, having rejected offers of marriage, was considered too old to be marriageable. She was working in London as a superintendent at The Hospital for Invalid Gentlewomen in Harley Street, yet in her personal life she continued to be stifled by her family's wishes, their overbearing disapproval and their social conditioning.

With the outbreak of the Crimean War in 1854, Nightingale found the summit of her vocation. Making use of her high social position and approaching friends within the government, she was permitted to take an expedition of female nurses (all volunteers) to run a military hospital at Scutari, on the shore of the Bosphorus. She was adored by the men she nursed and by the media who saw her as an angel of mercy. She became known as "the lady with the lamp" for making her ward rounds while carrying a lamp to check on her patients.

As soon as she reached Scutari, she was appalled by the hygiene standards and filth of the makeshift hospital, and immediately ordered 300 scrubbing brushes. She also sent an order back to London requesting 80 more nurses. Ironically, many of the men who had survived the battlefield were now dying of diseases caused by the two-day journey to the hospital and the diseases that were rife in the filthy hospital buildings.

Many historians now criticize Nightingale's medical record – for example her belief that infection arose from "miasma" or foul smells (although Nightingale was not the only Victorian medic to believe in the role of miasma in infection). Nightingale herself was forced to look at her own track record after returning home and realized that the numbers of men who had died in her hospital were enormous in comparison to other hospitals – this was largely due to the terrible siting of the hospital, the exhaustive journey to reach it and the disease-ridden sewers that ran beneath her wards.

There is, however, no questioning the positive impact that Florence Nightingale had on nursing – she promoted the need for good hygiene and increased the prescribed space between hospital beds (in the past they were crammed as close as possible, which allowed infection to spread through wards). The result was that nursing was turned into a serious profession. There is also no doubting how much she changed the Victorian perception of women, showing that they could be both capable and intelligent. Nightingale did much to help with the inexorable move forward towards gender equality.

I am admitted to Miss Nightingale's presence. A slight figure, in the nurses' dress; with a pale, gentle, and withal firm face, resting lightly in the palm of one white hand, while the other supports the elbow – a position which gives to her countenance a keen inquiring expression, which is rather marked. Standing thus in repose, and yet keenly observant ... was Florence Nightingale – that Englishwoman whose name shall never die, but sound like music on the lips of British men until the hour of doom. She has read Dr. F – – 's letter ... and asks, in her gentle but eminently practical and business-like way, "What do you want, Mrs. Seacole – anything that we can do for you? If it lies in my power, I shall be very happy."

From Mary Seacole's recollections of Scutari, published in *The Wonderful Adventures of Mrs Seacole in Many Lands*, 1857

(Florence Nightingale was not as flattering to Mary Seacole in return, probably out of jealousy – she said she did not approve of Seacole's British Hotel and later said that Mary had kept a "bad house" in the Crimea, the cause of "much drunkenness and improper conduct".)

I should have thought that no preface would have been required to introduce Mrs. Seacole to the British public.... If singleness of heart, true charity, and Christian works; if trials and sufferings, dangers and perils, encountered boldly by a helpless woman on her errand of mercy in the camp and in the battle-field, can excite sympathy or move curiosity, Mary Seacole will have many friends and many readers.

I have witnessed her devotion and her courage ... and I trust that England will not forget one who nursed her sick, who sought out her wounded to aid and succour them, and who performed the last offices for some of her illustrious dead.

From William Howard Russell's preface to *The Wonderful Adventures of Mrs Seacole in Many Lands*, 1857

MARY SEACOLE (1805–81)

Born Mary Jane Grant in Kingston, Jamaica, Mary's mother was a "free" Jamaican who ran a boarding house and was renowned as a "doctress", and her father was a Scottish army officer. In her autobiography, Mary described herself as "Creole". While in her twenties, she travelled to London for the first time, accompanied by a Jamaican friend. The two of them experienced regular abuse, but despite this hostility, Mary stayed for a year.

On her way home to Jamaica, Mary visited the Bahamas, Haiti and Cuba – and was on a ship that caught fire mid-ocean. In 1836, she married Edwin Horatio Hamilton Seacole, the godson of Lord Nelson. In 1843, a huge fire destroyed their home, so she and her husband went to live with her mother. Edwin died a year later, after eight years of marriage and terrible health, and Mary's mother died shortly afterwards. In 1850, a cholera epidemic swept through Jamaica, and Mary used the skills her mother had taught her to nurse people. In the same year, she travelled to Panama to join her brother, who was working there and had got himself into difficulties. While she was in Panama, a cholera epidemic broke out and the American doctor fled, so Mary took over his role and began nursing the sick. She caught cholera, but recovered and set up a café opposite her brother's shop. However, she became homesick and soon returned to Jamaica.

In 1853, yellow fever broke out in Jamaica and once more Mary cared for locals and for the British soldiers who went to her for help. When the British army heard about her skills, they asked her to come and nurse their sick in the army camp. In 1854, Mary travelled to England, wanting to help nurse the troops in the Crimea. She arrived with glowing references from friends in the British army, but was still rejected by the War Office because of the colour of her skin. Together with a Mr Thomas Day, a relation of her husband, she began fundraising and made enough money to travel out to the Crimea and set up the British Hotel. It was only two miles from Balaclava; Florence Nightingale's hospital was a two-day journey from the battlefields. Mary was the first woman to enter Sebastopol from the English lines and she was often seen riding onto the battlefield loaded with medical supplies (at risk of being shot by the Russians). The men she helped called her "Mother Seacole" or "Aunty Seacole". At the end of the war, Mary Seacole and Thomas Day were declared bankrupt. A fund was set up by grateful soldiers, letters were written to *The Times,* and a poem in support of Mary Seacole was published in *Punch.*

In 1857, her bankruptcy was written off and British courts declared she was no longer a debtor. Mary published her memoirs, *The Wonderful Adventures of Mrs Seacole in Many Lands*, and in July, a gala was held in her honour in Royal Surrey Gardens, London. More than 80,000 people were estimated to have attended. In 1873, Mary was appointed masseuse to the constantly ailing Princess of Wales, who suffered from severe neuralgia and a host of other medical complaints. Mary Seacole died in May 1881 after a long illness.

╔══╗

THE SCRAMBLE FOR AFRICA

- In 1876, King Leopold II of Belgium – on hearing about the rich mineral deposits in the Congo Basin – created the International African Association. His aim was to take control of the Congo.
- The Berlin Conference was convened by Otto von Bismarck in 1884–85. Its aim was to discuss the future of Africa, and its supposed intention was the "suppression of slavery". Thirteen European powers attended the conference. King Leopold II pushed for his "property claims" in Africa to be sanctioned and was eventually granted land in the Congo as the Congo Free State (also known as the Belgian Congo).
- This provided the catalyst for other European powers to start grabbing land in Africa and carving out the entire continent into sections ruled by European countries. The only African countries to remain independent were Ethiopia and Liberia.
- The scramble for Africa continued until the outbreak of the First World War in 1914.

╚══╝

THE INDIAN MUTINY

In May 1857, soldiers in the Bengal Army shot dead their British officers. These soldiers then marched on Delhi, and the revolutionary fever quickly spread to Indian civilians. There was an upsurge of violence against the occupying British, and hundreds of settlers – including women and children, as the newspapers were quick to point out – were slaughtered by the angry Indian rebels. However, neither the British military nor the British media attempted to understand why the rebellion had taken place.

The rebellion had begun after rumours began circulating amongst the Hindu and Muslim soldiers about the new type of rifle they had been issued with. It was said that the cartridges they needed to use were greased with animal fat, specifically with pig lard (forbidden in the Muslim diet) and cow fat (cows are sacred in Hinduism). When the soldiers asked if the rumours were true, the British military commanders – who had no interest in local religions – refused to discuss the issue.

Despite the many years of British occupation in India, the vast majority of British settlers had no understanding of the local culture.

The mutiny lasted for over a year and led to the downfall of the British East India Company and of the Mughal Empire, with the last Mughal emperor sent by the British into exile in Burma (he had been accused of starting the revolt, even though his role was minimal). The war ostensibly came to an end in June of 1858, although battles still raged in parts of India for another year. It did not bring about an end to British rule in India, but it changed the way both British and Indian communities regarded the "British Raj". The British military leaders also began to recruit men from other areas, bringing soldiers from Gurkha regiments as well as Sikh soldiers into the British army.

BOER WAR FACTS

- In 1877, the British annexed part of the Transvaal region of South Africa, which had already been annexed in the 1850s by Dutch settlers known as Boers.
- The name "Boer" comes from the Dutch word for "farmer".
- The First Boer War began in December of 1880, when the Boers rose up against the new British occupiers.
- Ironically, the most popular weapon used by the Boers in the war of 1880–81 was the Westley Richards rifle, which was manufactured in Britain.
- For centuries, the British army had been recognizable by their red uniforms, but it was realized during the first Boer War how conspicuous they were on a battlefield and how easy it was to target them. In the Second Boer War, the soldiers wore cool cotton uniforms in a khaki colour, which soldiers in India had been wearing since the 1880s.
- The Pretoria Convention of 1881 gave the Boers some rights, but kept the Transvaal under British supervisory control.
- The London Convention of 1884 gave the power back to the Boers in what was now the South African Republic.
- During 1886, gold was discovered in the Transvaal.
- In 1896, the Jameson Raid – in which Cecil Rhodes attempted to overthrow the Transvaal government – failed.

- The Second Boer War broke out on 11 October 1899 over British attempts to gain control of what the Boers saw as their territory – at this date, neither one of the colonial occupiers was concerned about the rights of the indigenous inhabitants of South Africa to the land and its resources.
- The Orange Free State allied with the Transvaal Boers.
- The British army was bolstered by soldiers from other colonies, including Australia, Canada and New Zealand.
- Initially the Boers seemed to be winning the war. However, by 1900 events started to change – the British promised protection to any Boer fighters who wished to surrender and fight for them instead, and a large number of Boer soldiers defected.
- Between 1900 and 1902, the fighting intensified and guerrilla tactics began to be used on both sides. Many Africans with no loyalties to either side became casualties as the land was fought over and often burnt and ruined by retreating troops.
- The idea of the "concentration camp" had been used effectively by the Spanish and the US army in recent years, and the British began using them to incarcerate the Boers and local Africans (who were often used as slave labour to help the war effort on both sides).
- At the end of 1900, the British social reformer Emily Hobhouse set sail for South Africa after hearing terrible stories of abuse. (Nineteenth-century concentration camps were vile places, but they were intended as places of imprisonment rather than extermination, as those created by the Nazis in the Second World War would become.) The report she delivered to the British government about the poor administration of the camps and the resultant agonies suffered by the prisoners shamed the government into changing its military policies.
- The Second Boer War came to an end on 31 May 1902, with the signing of the Peace of Vereeniging. (This was during the reign of King Edward VII in Britain.)

I call this camp system a wholesale cruelty… To keep these Camps going is murder to the children.

From "Report of a Visit to the Camps of Women and Children in the Cape and Orange River Colonies" by Emily Hobhouse, June 1901

BRITISH EXPLORERS AND ADVENTURERS
OF THE VICTORIAN AGE

John Franklin (1786–1847)
William Penny (1808–92)
David Livingstone (1813–73)
Richard Burton (1821–90)
John Hanning Speke (1827–64)
George Strong Nares (1831–1915)
Isabella Bird (1832–1904)
Wilfrid Scawen Blunt (1840–1922)
Florence, Lady Baker (1841–1916)
Mary Kingsley (1862–1900)
Lady Anne Savile (1864–1927)
Gertrude Bell (1868–1926)
Robert Falcon Scott (1868–1912)
Ernest Henry Shackleton (1874–1922)

11

HOSPITALS AND HEALTHCARE

At the start of the nineteenth century, there were voluntary hospitals, which were entirely dependent on charitable donations, and there were workhouse infirmaries. Everyone else was nursed at home, either by a family member or a paid nurse (many of whom had no proper training or qualifications). For many, hospitals were regarded as terrifying places known to be full of disease. Those people who had no choice but to go into hospital (usually because they had no one to care for them at home or because they had an infectious disease that their family was at risk of catching) were expected to die there.

LIFE EXPECTANCY

In Victorian Britain, the average lifespan for a middle-class man was 45. Of the country's poorest people, those who lived in the country survived longer than those who lived in towns. One report showed that indigent country dwellers lived twice as long as their urban counterparts.

In the mid-Victorian era, one in five children died before their fifth birthday. In the most crowded urban areas, infant mortality rose to one in three.

⛧ One of the best places for hospital care during the nineteenth century was Edinburgh, because it had such a well-respected medical school. There had been so many medical students in Edinburgh during the eighteenth century, that, long before Queen Victoria came to the throne, hospitals were more plentiful in Scotland than elsewhere in the United Kingdom.

MEDICAL TREATMENT

At the start of Queen Victoria's reign, operations were crude and usually carried out in insanitary conditions. There was little understanding of hygiene, and anaesthesia had not yet been invented. Alcohol was used both as a painkiller for the patient and to swab the area to be operated on in an attempt to minimize infection. As the opium trade began to grow, opiates became popular forms of pain relief. Despite improvements in infection understanding and control, operations remained extremely dangerous undertakings.

Throughout the early years of the Victorian age, voluntary hospitals were entirely at the mercy of their benefactors, who, with no medical training, outranked the doctors. Admissions to hospital could not be agreed by a doctor but only by the board of benefactors. By the 1860s, this practice had been changed and doctors were finally permitted to make medical decisions without first checking with the patrons. Most doctors in voluntary hospitals were not paid for their time. They would have owned their own private practices, and many preferred to charge high fees to private patients, thereby enabling them to work at the voluntary hospitals for free.

By the 1860s, more hospitals had been set up to cater properly for all medical needs. The wealthy had started to realize that they could pay for proper hospital care and that the conditions inside a professional hospital were far more suitable for operations and serious medical treatment than a bedroom at home.

Before the advent of the National Health Service in the twentieth century, being ill could be extremely expensive. Seeing a doctor cost money, as did paying for medicine. If a sick person was of working age, he or she would lose their salary for the duration of their illness; this had terrible repercussions for a family's income. Added to that, if someone was needed to nurse the patient, they also lost income and risked losing their job as a result of taking time off work. Many of the country's poorest people earned just enough to stay alive, so an illness in the family could prove the tipping point in their finances and often led to families being evicted for non-payment of rent. Illness was one of the reasons why people ended up in the workhouse.

CHILDBIRTH AND MATERNITY CARE

Throughout the nineteenth century, the role of the midwife was not regulated. The first Midwives Act was not passed until 1902 (during the reign of King Edward VII). Women in labour were attended by friends or family members (usually experienced women who had children of their own), a doctor if they could afford one, or a "monthly nurse" (women who were paid to attend a childbirth). Monthly nurses had no formal training and were often derided as disreputable (most famously as depicted in Dickens's *Martin Chuzzlewit* in the form of Mrs Gamp). Being a monthly nurse involved a great deal of dirty and menial work – as well as assisting at childbirth (known as "lying in"), these women were also called upon to "lay out" the dead. The two professions were closely allied, as maternal and infant mortality were a constant threat in every pregnancy.

Many Victorian women who survived childbirth went on to die of puerperal fever or "childbed fever", which meant an infection contracted after the birth itself (because of the lack of understanding about hygiene). Many women also died as a result of lack of understanding about how important it was to ensure the removal of the placenta after the birth.

For those women and babies who survived the ordeal, the monthly nurse stayed on for around a month (hence the name) after the birth. During this time, the mother was expected to stay in bed and the nurse would care for both her and her child, sleeping next to the baby at night and taking him or her to the mother at feeding times.

THE FLORA HASTINGS SCANDAL

During the last years of the reign of King William IV, a young woman named Flora Hastings was sent to live with the Duchess of Kent, to be her daughter Princess Victoria's companion. When Victoria became queen, Flora Hastings was made one of her ladies-in-waiting. Despite

SPECIALIST HOSPITALS

The following hospitals opened during the reign of Queen Victoria:

- 1838 – The Ear, Nose and Throat Hospital opened in London, one of the first specialist hospitals in Britain
- 1847 – The Queen's hospital in Birmingham
- 1851 – The Free Cancer Hospital in Westminster, London
- 1852 – The Hospital for Sick Children in Great Ormond Street, London
- 1859 – The first "cottage hospital" (small rural hospital) opened in Cranleigh in Sussex. Over the following two decades, another 147 cottage hospitals were founded.
- 1866 – The Victoria Hospital for Sick Children in Kensington, London
- 1866 – The Bristol Royal Hospital for Women and Children
- 1881 – Rubery Hill Asylum in Birmingham
- 1887 – The London Skin Hospital
- 1890 – Victoria Hospital at Langside, Glasgow

QUACK CURES

Even though medical care was becoming much more professional, "quack" doctors were always ready to sell their dubious products – most such "cures" were advertised in newspapers and sold by mail order. In 1859, the following testimonial appeared regularly in newspapers countrywide and was typical advertising of the day:

A surprising cure of asthma of 18 years standing with wasting of flesh…. "To Mr. Lambert, chemist, 20 Jermyn-street, Haymarket, London. – Sir, it is with the greatest pleasure that I write to thank you for the wonderful benefit I have derived by taking Lambert's Asthmatic Balsam, which has completely cured me of an asthma of 18 years standing…. The first dose gave me relief a few minutes after taking it, and in a few weeks by it, with the blessing of God, I was restored to health and strength. I am now as robust as I was when thirty years of age."

the five years of companionship, Queen Victoria turned against Flora very publicly two years after she came to the throne.

In early 1839, Flora began to complain of stomach pains and sickness. Her stomach began to swell, and gossips whispered that the unmarried lady-in-waiting must be pregnant. Queen Victoria began to believe the rumours despite Flora's protestations to the contrary. As Victoria noted in her journals, Flora's swollen stomach was "exceedingly suspicious"; the Queen was convinced that there was a child and that the father was Sir John Conroy. He was a close confidante and rumoured lover of Victoria's mother, the Duchess of Kent. Conroy was also a bullying man whom Victoria had despised since childhood.

In order not to lose her place at court, Flora Hastings was forced to undergo a medical examination by two male doctors. Both doctors reported that there was no pregnancy and never had been one, and signed a certificate to attest to it. The rumours persisted and the Queen was now at the head of the rumour-mongers. The Hastings family demanded a public apology – which they were denied. Flora wrote to an influential uncle who was living in Paris. She told him every sordid detail and he decided to send the story to a popular newspaper, *The Examiner*. The story was instantly a cause célèbre. The public and members of the court debated it hotly, and people began to blame the Queen for her role, some accusing her of having started the rumours herself. Public opinion was so high that the Queen was horrified to be hissed at by crowds during public engagements.

Flora was unable to enjoy the huge public support, as her health was deteriorating rapidly. She lost weight at an alarming rate and her hair began to fall out. The Queen went to visit her and recorded that Flora was "as thin as anybody can be who is still alive, literally a skeleton". Flora died a few days later, but before her death she insisted that a post mortem should be carried out on her corpse. The post mortem found that Flora had died of a diseased liver, the early symptoms of which had been the distended belly and sickness that the Queen had insisted were signs of a pregnancy. The prime minister, Lord Melbourne, was such close friends with the Queen that public opinion had also turned against him. On the day of Flora Hastings's funeral, he was so worried about the possibility of rioting that he ordered the streets on which the funeral cortege would travel to be lined with police.

˙CHOLERA

A new outbreak of cholera, known as "the blue death" (in reference to the dreaded plague or "black death"), occurred in London in 1854. It was to prove even more deadly than previous outbreaks.

Dr John Snow (the doctor who had gained notoriety when he gave Queen Victoria chloroform during the birth of Prince Leopold) was the man who made the most important breakthrough in the fight against cholera. In 1854, he described the outbreak as "the most terrible outbreak of cholera which ever occurred in this kingdom". Although his theories were widely criticized initially, Snow had become convinced that cholera was not airborne, as was widely believed at the time, but waterborne. He was trying to assist the community around Broad Street, in a cramped and filthy part of the London district of Soho, where over 500 people died within 10 days. Snow, who lived in a more salubrious area of Soho, was desperate to make the medical breakthrough needed to stop the epidemic. He began to plot on a map the places where deaths had occurred and noticed that at the centre of all of them was the water pump on Broad Street.

Snow began badgering the local health authority to disable the pump. Eventually the pump handle was removed, which caused fury amongst the local people. When the water supply was inspected, it was discovered that the well from which the water was being drawn was running alongside cesspools from the slums and nearby houses, as well as the rudimentary sewage system of Soho.

Despite the fact that Snow's work led directly to a cessation of the cholera outbreak, fellow medics ridiculed his work. In 1855, the medical journal *The Lancet* (whose editor was famed for his antipathy towards Snow) published an editorial about Snow's cholera research, which included the phrase "Has he any facts to show in proof? No!". Snow's essay "On the Mode of the Communication of Cholera" was also poorly reviewed. When he died in 1858, Snow's obituary in *The Lancet* omitted any mention of his achievements on cholera research and it was not until the 1880s that the medical world finally began to take his findings seriously.

CHOLERA PREVENTION

In the 1830s, public advertisements advised the following procedures to help prevent cholera:

1. Let every person be washed perfectly clean, morning and evening.
2. Let every room be cleaned and swept every day, and well washed at least once a week.
3. Let no rubbish nor dirt lie about the door, nor near the house.
4. Let off all stagnant water.
5. Let the house be whitewashed with hot lime.
6. Beware of Drunkenness – nothing is so likely to bring on Disease.

If anyone is seized with sickness, slight vomiting, and purging, a burning heat at the stomach, with cramp in various parts of the body, and a feeling of cold all over, it probably is the Cholera.

⤶ Victorian Health Tips

In 1884, the International Health Exhibition was held in London. Dr Jaeger extolled the virtues of warm woollen underclothing, and lectures, displays and stalls gave tips about diet and lifestyle. There was great excitement about the radical vegetarian restaurant at the exhibition.

LUNATIC ASYLUMS

For centuries, mental illnesses of all types had been labelled "insanity" and patients were treated with cruelty and derision. By the Victorian age, the era of the "village idiot" or royal "fool" was outdated, but the treatment was equally cruel and archaic. The term "lunatic" (which actually meant a person driven mad by the forces of the moon) encompassed anyone who fell outside the norms of society. It was used to refer to any person with a mental or physical disability (all of whom were shunned in Victorian Britain), women who had sex outside of marriage (which included victims of rape), political agitators, atheists and anyone who refused to conform. Poor people were more in danger of being incarcerated for insanity than wealthy people, and women were much more likely to be imprisoned in a "lunatic asylum" than men.

BEDLAM

The most famous asylum in Britain was London's Royal Bethlem Hospital, commonly known as "Bedlam". Still in existence today as a research and treatment centre, it is one of the oldest psychiatric hospitals in the world, having been founded in 1247. Initially it was intended as a refuge for the homeless, but soon had become known as an asylum for the "mad". Until the mid-nineteenth century, patients were chained up, beaten for perceived misbehaviour, and looked upon as objects of entertainment. Visitors could pay to visit the asylum and watch the inmates as though they were wild animals in a zoo.

A new way of treating the "insane" began to be mooted during the early Victorian period, and in 1853 a new superintendent was appointed to the Royal Bethlem Hospital; his name was W. Charles Hood. He was determined to make the hospital a more humane setting, favouring more "enlightened principles" in what would later become known as the field of psychiatry. One of Hood's most important actions was to ban the use of the iron manacles, by which patients had previously been restrained and chained to the walls. Instead, patients considered a danger to themselves or to others began to be confined in rooms with padded walls, or were medicated with sedatives.

CHLOROFORM

In 1853, Queen Victoria made history when she asked to have chloroform to alleviate the pain of childbirth. It was used during the birth of her eighth child, Prince Leopold, and the media and medical establishment were both highly critical of Dr John Snow's decision to allow it. When it was discovered, some years later, that the prince was a haemophiliac, many people claimed that it was because of the circumstances of his birth. Angry religious campaigners pointed to the book of Genesis in the Bible, which stated that women should "bear children in intense pain and suffering". The use of chloroform in childbirth was seen as going against God's will (there were no similar protests against chloroform when it came to men having operations).

LEECHES

Up until the late nineteenth century, leeches were used as a medical aid. Many doctors believed that illness was caused by infected blood, or by too much blood in the body, so they prescribed leeches to suck out the infected blood. Patients often died as a result of the treatment.

QUALIFIED DOCTORS

In 1858, a new law was passed to ensure that the medical profession would improve. Until now, it had been easy for a man to set himself up as a medical practitioner, even without a medical degree. From 1858 onwards, only qualified men could practise as doctors. From 1876, women were also permitted to train as doctors, thanks to the work of Elizabeth Garrett Andersen.

Elizabeth Garrett (1836–1917) grew up in an unusual Victorian home, where her parents encouraged all of their daughters to have careers and independence. Unfortunately society was not as forward thinking as the Garrett household and Elizabeth, who wanted to be a doctor, was told that she was eligible only – by dint of her gender – to train as a nurse. Alongside her nursing studies, Elizabeth attended medical students' classes, until the other students (all male) complained and had her banned from them. Having completed as much medical training in Britain as the authorities would allow, in 1865 she sat for the Society of Apothecaries exam. The society had not had the forethought to ban female entrants – Garrett passed and the medical authorities were forced to acknowledge her as the first female doctor in Britain. The Society of Apothecaries rapidly changed its rules to ban female students from taking the exam in the future.

In 1866, Elizabeth set up a hospital for women, in London, and began campaigning for a change in the law to permit women to train as doctors. In the meantime, she taught herself French and travelled to France, where she passed medical exams, but despite having attained a medical degree in Paris, she was still not permitted entry to the British Medical Registry.

In 1874, Garrett helped to found the London School of Medicine for Women. Two years later, her campaigning zeal paid off and an Act was passed that permitted women to enter the medical professions. In 1883, she was permitted to become dean of the hospital she had helped to found in 1874. She had also found the time to marry, in 1871, and have three children. Her daughter Louisa Garrett Anderson also became a doctor.

⚑ The young Elizabeth Garrett Anderson was inspired to follow a medical career after meeting Dr Elizabeth Blackwell, the first woman to graduate as a doctor in the USA. In the 1870s, Elizabeth Garrett Anderson gave Elizabeth Blackwell the job of professor of Gynaecology at her new London School of Medicine for Women.

NURSING

When Queen Victoria came to the throne, the world of nursing was not regulated and nurses did not require qualifications. Most nursing was carried out in the home, usually by women and girls. From an early age, girls learnt how to take care of their younger siblings as well as ill family members. Many households clung to the practices in *Buchan's Domestic Medicine*, a book originally published by the doctor William Buchan in the 1790s and reissued in 1848. It included advice on illnesses being caused by night air, by having wet feet or by eating "cold" foods, such as cucumbers and watery fruits like melon.

In the 1840s, the first formal nursing schools began to be taken seriously in Britain, and in the 1850s nursing became recognized as a respectable profession, primarily thanks to the pioneering work of Florence Nightingale.

⚑ Following Louis Pasteur's 1864 discovery that infections were caused by germs, the Glaswegian surgeon Joseph Lister began experimenting with new ways to prevent infection. One of his methods was to keep spraying his operating room with a fine mist of carbolic (a disinfectant).

12

CLOTHING AND FASHION

One of the great breakthroughs in Victorian clothing was the arrival of cotton. As the factories grew ever more adept at producing cotton goods, it wasn't only fashions that changed, but also public health. Prior to this time, even on the hottest days and in the most punishing of hot working conditions, most people had been forced to wear wool; the arrival of cotton made clothing much more hygienic, and it could be washed much more easily.

RICH AND POOR

Fashions changed quickly and radically – but only for the country's wealthiest people. Dresses were often made up of separate sections, such as detachable sleeves or changeable bodices, meaning that women could update their clothes without having to buy an entire new dress. Most young women, outside of the upper classes, knew how to sew, mend and decorate their own clothes and accessories.

THE RATIONAL DRESS SOCIETY

In 1881, the Rational Dress Society was founded. Its manifesto ran:

The Rational Dress Society protests against the introduction of any fashion in dress that either deforms the figure, impedes the movements of the body, or in any way tends to injure the health. It protests against the wearing of tightly fitting corsets; of high-heeled shoes; of heavily weighted skirts, as rendering healthy exercise almost impossible; and of all tie down cloaks or other garments impeding on the movements of the arms. It protests against crinolines or crinolettes of any kind as ugly and deforming....[It] requires all to be dressed healthily, comfortably, and beautifully, to seek what conduces to birth, comfort and beauty in our dress as a duty to ourselves and each other.

WHITE WEDDINGS

At the start of Victoria's reign, it was not expected that a wedding dress would be white. Although it became popular after the Queen wore a white wedding dress, the fashion did not become widespread until the 1870s. For the majority of British women, the idea of wearing a dress only once would have been unthinkable. A wedding dress was expected to be a pretty dress that could be worn again and again.

DEADLY FASHIONS

- On 22 October 1844, a young Scottish woman named Jane Goodwin died very suddenly. According to the Dundee Courier, her death was the result of her corset being too tightly laced.
- There were numerous newspaper reports of "death by crinoline". One such death, in January 1861, occurred when a young London woman named Miss Maria Power attempted to put a tilting candle upright. The flame ignited her dress and then her cage crinoline – made of wood – caught fire. As women had crinolines tied on to them, by maids or sisters, it was impossible to get out of them without help. The young woman pulled down silk curtains and wrapped herself in them, but they also caught fire. The coroner later noted that the crinoline had prevented almost any damage to the lower part of the woman's body, but had raged with such heat that it had burnt her upper half beyond saving.

BATHING

Sea bathing grew in popularity during the nineteenth century and so-called "bathing dresses" were created. These were frequently made of wool and were difficult to swim in. Men and women usually swam from different beaches (men and boys swam naked), but women and girls still had to be elaborately covered up. A woman would walk fully clothed into a bathing hut. Inside she would change into her bathing dress (helped by the bathing-hut attendant), and the hut would then trundle on rails to the edge of the sea. The woman could emerge directly into the sea and return to the hut to change back into her clothes. Sunbathing was not popular for most of the century as the only white women with tanned skin were farm labourers who had no choice but to work outside.

MEN'S CLOTHING

During the time of the Prince Regent and his reign as King George IV, men's clothing had been flamboyant and brightly coloured, and fashionable men were known as "beaux". To be known as a "beau", such as the famous Beau Brummel, was seen as a great honour. By the late 1830s, however, men's fashion had become much less flamboyant. Throughout most of the Victorian era, British men had little choice but to dress in sombre colours.

Victorian gentlemen would not be seen in public without wearing a waistcoat over their shirt, as well as a coat, hat and gloves. Even on the hottest days of the year, taking off one's coat or hat in public was unacceptable. It was only working-class men and labourers who were expected to be seen with their shirt sleeves visible.

While men's suits were expected to be sombre in colour, one of the few articles that was often brightly coloured was the waistcoat – especially when silk from China and India became more widespread. Too bright a waistcoat, however, was considered "vulgar". Fashionable men could also show more of their personality by choosing a brightly coloured silk cravat (worn around the neck).

In the second half of Victoria's reign, the most fashionable type of man's coat was the "frock coat"; instead of being straight, these coats had full skirts, usually intended to stop at the knee. Trousers were worn with very high, fitted waists, and were closed with buttons. Although the first recognizable "zip" had been shown at the Great Exhibition in 1851, it was not taken seriously until the 1890s and did not become popular until well into the twentieth century. Victorian men did not wear belts; instead, loose-fitting trousers were held up by braces.

By the 1880s, fashion-conscious men were adhering to the new Aesthetic style of dressing, in which clothes allowed for more freedom of movement. Whereas suits had been carefully tailored before now, these "sack suits" were roomier.

CHILDREN

Children were dressed like miniature adults, with little consideration of what clothes would be suitable for playing in. Boys and girls wore dresses and petticoats at least until they were fully potty trained; it was common for nannies in wealthy families to keep their male charges wearing dresses until they were around five years old. Girls and boys both wore shorter versions of adult clothing, with girls being permitted to show their ankles and boys wearing shorts instead of trousers (even in cold weather). Sailor suits became very popular for boys and girls following the publication of Frances Hodgson Burnett's novel *Little Lord Fauntleroy* in 1886. A new fashion began of dressing boys in "Fauntleroy suits" of velvet trimmed with large lace collars.

Boys were considered to be growing up when they were out of "short trousers", and girls to be growing up when they started wearing long skirts and wore their hair pinned up instead of leaving it down (usually in ribbons). Adult women were not expected to ever wear their hair loose in public; when the Pre-Raphaelite Brotherhood painted portraits of women with long, flowing hair, their pictures were considered overtly sexual.

And then the Earl looked up. What Cedric saw was a large old man with shaggy white hair and eyebrows, and a nose like an eagle's beak between his deep, fierce eyes. What the Earl saw was a graceful, childish figure in a black velvet suit, with a lace collar, and with love-locks waving about the handsome, manly little face, whose eyes met his with a look of innocent good-fellowship. If the Castle was like the palace in a fairy story, it must be owned that little Lord Fauntleroy

*was himself rather like a small copy of the fairy prince,
though he was not at all aware of the fact, and perhaps was
rather a sturdy young model of a fairy.*

From *Little Lord Fauntleroy* by Frances Hodgson Burnett, 1886

FASHION INDUSTRY WORKERS

Many people who worked in the fashion trade worked extremely long hours for very little pay. Most of them ruined their health, especially their eyesight and their posture, by working hunched over in poor lighting.

In 1881, Portsmouth's *The Evening News* printed a story made shocking not by the content but by the writer's utter lack of compassion:

*Cuckoo advises its readers to give up wearing clothes. At any
rate, they ought first to find out where they are made. A case
has just been made public of a tailor employed by 'a good
firm' being found making and repairing clothes in a room
with one child lying ill with small-pox in it – and another
lying dead from the same awful disease! It is very long indeed
since we have read a more shocking disclosure. Scarlet fever
in milk, trichinae in pork, arsenic in wall paper, typhus fever
in drains – these and all the rest are bad, but small-pox from
our clothes sent out to be repaired is a sickening terror.*

In his children's fairytale *The Happy Prince* (1888), Oscar Wilde made one of his main characters a poor seamstress. The protagonist is a statue of a wealthy prince, plated in gold and decorated with precious jewels, which stands high above the city. The real prince was happy in his lifetime, but now as a statue he looks over the city and sees the misery and poverty that he was too ignorant and busy to care about during his privileged life. The statue befriends a swallow and tells him of the things he is haunted by:

*Far away in a little street there is a poor house. One of the
windows is open, and through it I can see a woman seated
at a table. Her face is thin and worn, and she has coarse,
red hands, all pricked by the needle, for she is a seamstress.*

She is embroidering passion-flowers on a satin gown for the loveliest of the Queen's maids-of-honour to wear at the next Court-ball. In a bed in the corner of the room her little boy is lying ill. He has a fever, and is asking for oranges. His mother has nothing to give him but river water, so he is crying. Swallow, Swallow, little Swallow, will you not bring her the ruby out of my sword-hilt? My feet are fastened to this pedestal and I cannot move.

WHALE SLAUGHTER

The Victorians were responsible for a wholesale slaughter of whales, which were coveted for the spermaceti oil that was used for candle-making and lamp oil, and for the "whalebone" that was essential for making corsets. Despite its name, whalebone is not actually bone – it is the baleen (or mouth plates) of baleen whales, which is composed of very strong keratin. The baleen was manipulated into shape and then boiled to make it hard and fixed, so that shape would remain solid no matter what the corset-wearer did.

FEATHERED FASHION

In 1898, one of the country's most popular artists George Frederic Watts exhibited his latest campaigning masterpiece. The oil painting, entitled *A Dedication*, shows an angel covering its face and weeping over a plinth holding the dismembered parts of birds. The plinth is carved with the image of an evil-looking figure, smiling greedily. The painting was accompanied by the dedication: "To all those who love the beautiful and mourn over the senseless and cruel destruction of bird life and beauty."

This painting, which also became known by the title of *The Shuddering Angel*, was Watts's reaction to the prevalent fashion for wearing not only feathers but also sometimes whole wings or entire stuffed birds; he was horrified to see women walking around with several slaughtered birds on their hats. A year before Watts exhibited his painting, the Society for the Protection of Birds (SPB), had sent out a letter to the newspapers and public bodies "calling attention to the continued destruction of beautiful and useful birds at the dictates of fashion". Although there had been calls for change for several years, the fashion continued and there was especial outrage following the Queen's 1897 jubilee when a number of women in the royal procession were observed wearing dead birds on their heads: "From princess to peasant the evil is rampant. On Jubilee Day the hearts of many bird lovers were made sick with disgust at seeing head after head in our beloved Queen's procession decorated by plumes obtainable only at breeding season, meaning a cruel destruction of parent birds and a miserable death by slow starvation to helpless nestlings." Watts was a member of the SPB and had begun his painting to chime with its campaign.

> *The ladies who wear feathers in their hats do not take their act so seriously as Mr. Watts does, and ... some of them will only smile when they find a great artist taking the trouble to paint a majestic angel weeping — over what? Over a shelf-ful of the wings of birds! It is a little startling to read so severe a sermon, and from such a quarter, over an offence which well-meaning people commit in all unconsciousness.*
>
> **From *The Times*, 1899**

FASHION IN PREGNANCY

Visibly pregnant women of the middle and upper classes were not expected to be seen in public, and fashion houses and in particular corset-makers devised ways in which women could disguise their pregnancies. It didn't matter if a woman was respectably married and everyone knew she was expecting a baby, it was the shape of a baby bump that was deemed offensive. Maternity corsets promised pregnant women a waist, even in their third trimester of pregnancy. They were made to fit over the bump and then tightly laced to create as small a waist as possible, thanks to complicated rows of buckles and straps as well as boning. Women in late pregnancy could also wear an abdomen belt to keep the bump suppressed. Doctors warned against all these fashions, knowing that they often resulted in miscarriage, birth complications or infant and maternal death. However, society decreed that pregnancy was an unnatural thing to look at, and women were forced to comply or remain hidden away at home.

13

CHILDHOOD

Life for a Victorian child varied widely depending on their financial and social circumstances. Children from wealthy families were dressed up like miniature adults in fine clothes and were not allowed to get dirty. They were looked after by servants and seldom saw their parents throughout the day – it was fully expected that they should be "seen and not heard". Children from poor families had to work from a very young age, because salaries for the poorest people were so low that most working-class adults could not afford to support a family on what they earned. Perhaps it was children from the new "middle classes" who had the most enviable existence of all the classes: they saw more of their parents (partly because the family could not afford so many servants), and did not have to work for a living.

> *Games for children should be provided out of doors as much as possible whenever the weather will allow. Running and playing come more natural to children than walking, and in these days of high-pressure education it is most essential that when released from the schoolroom they should find healthy, active exercise, and games which try the muscles instead of the brains.*
>
> **The Book of Household Management by Mrs Isabella Beeton, 1861**

Physical punishment was considered normal for Victorian children, who were regularly beaten by their parents or nannies.

TOYS

Once the manufacturing industry moved into the world of toy making, the types of toys seen in Victorian homes began to change. Whereas toys in the past had all been handmade and usually simple, factories now began churning out much more complicated items, such as clockwork toys, furniture for dolls' houses, children's tea sets, miniature shops complete with mini-branded products to be sold, rocking horses and train sets (which changed just as real train technology improved). Children were usually forbidden to play with toys on Sundays, unless their games had a religious purpose.

Victorian toys were mostly made of wood, cloth, paper or metal. Popular toys included paper cut-out dolls that could be dressed up in a variety of paper outfits, hoops, balls, spinning tops, skipping ropes, card games, stuffed animals, wooden sets of farmhouse animals, whole platoons of painted metal soldiers (the paint contained lead, which was not yet understood to be poisonous), building bricks, alphabet bricks and the new fashion for children's books. In the past, there had been very few books written specially for children, and those that did exist were usually dull and moralizing religious stories. In the nineteenth century, new writers such as Robert Louis Stevenson, Frances Hodgson Burnett, Lewis Carroll, Edward Lear, Charles Dickens, Oscar Wilde and Edith Nesbit began publishing stories – including short stories in newspapers – aimed specifically at children.

POPULAR VICTORIAN GAMES

Blindman's Buff • Charades • Chess • Cribbage • Happy Families • Hunt the Thimble • Jacks • Marbles • Pass the Slipper • Skittles • Snap • Squeak • Piggy • Squeak • Tag • Tom Tiddler's Ground

---

SPORTS

Boys were encouraged to play sports more than girls were (girls were expected to pursue indoor activities, such as music, embroidery and keeping a scrapbook). Both boys and girls were able to go out walking, to play croquet and to ride – although girls were expected to ride side-saddle. More energetic sports such as cricket, football and rugby were solely masculine pursuits. By the end of the nineteenth century, larger numbers of girls were being permitted to play tennis or golf, and sea bathing was recommended for both genders.

SCHOOLING

By the mid-Victorian age, it was usual for boys and girls of the middle and upper classes to receive a good or adequate education. Boys were usually educated at school and girls taught at home (either by their mother or by a governess). Boys who were educated at home – usually those who were in poor health and considered unable to cope with the rigours of school life – were taught by a tutor or "governor".

RAGGED SCHOOLS

The person credited with creating the first "ragged school" was a Portsmouth philanthropist named John Pounds. In 1818, he started offering an education to poor children he saw working on the streets. Pounds was not a rich man – he was a cobbler by profession – but he taught without charging a fee because he wanted to use his education to help children escape from the poverty trap. Other educational pioneers offering similar schemes included Sheriff Watson in Aberdeen, Thomas Cranfield in London and Kent, and Quintin Hogg in London.

In 1844, Lord Shaftesbury set up the Ragged School Union – a charity supported by many of his wealthy friends – which provided free schooling for poor children (who were usually dressed in ragged clothes, hence the name). Within a few years, around 200 ragged schools had been set up around Britain. It was soon realized, however, that without properly qualified teachers, these schools were doomed to failure. Over the next three decades, increasing numbers of educationalists began campaigning for proper, free education for all. This culminated in the 1870 Education Act.

IMPORTANT EDUCATION ACTS

- The 1870 Education Act was the first piece of legislation in Britain to deal specifically with education. It ensured that schools would be provided nationally and that high standards of teaching could be expected in all regions. Voluntary schools, such as the ragged schools, could continue, but the Act established the first local boards of education, which were given powers to build new schools and manage all the schools in their region.
- In 1876 a Royal Commission report for the Factory Acts suggested that the best way to stop exploitative child labour would be to make education compulsory for all children.
- The Education Act of 1880 built on the work of the Royal Commission and made it compulsory for children between the ages of five and 10 to attend school. This did not prevent children from working outside these hours.
- In 1893, the minimum school-leaving age was raised to 11, and was extended to include all deaf and blind children (who had previously been ignored).
- In 1899, the minimum school leaving age was again raised, to 12, and was extended to include all children with physical disabilities.

NANNIES

Upper-class and some middle-class children were raised mostly by a nanny, a servant whose sole job it was to take care of the children. In some families, the nanny became a substitute mother, and often stayed with the family for decades, looking after several generations of the same family. Nannies were usually unmarried women without children of their own, or widows with grown-up children (married women were not expected to work and found it very hard to find employment).

JOBS DONE BY VICTORIAN CHILDREN

Factory work, agricultural labouring, mining, caring for younger children, caring for the elderly, laundry, working as a domestic servant, working on market stalls, street sweeping, sweeping chimneys, making hats (millinery), sewing, catching vermin, pure collecting (scooping up animal excrement, known as "pure", from the streets to be used for leather tanning and in other industries), being apprenticed to a trade, prostitution.

APPRENTICES

In 1788, a law had been passed specifying that the youngest age at which a child could be taken on as an apprentice was eight, but this was almost universally ignored. Throughout the early years of Queen Victoria's reign, philanthropists and politicians began calling for a change in the laws that governed children's lives, and a large number of charitable committees were set up to campaign on behalf of those who had no political voice of their own. An apprentice was someone whose parents or guardians had paid for them to be instructed in a profession, under the guidance of a "master". Legal apprenticeships were bound by a contract, the usual term of which was seven years. There were many informal apprenticeships, which were not protected by law and which often led to abuse.

CHIMNEY SWEEPS

In 1834, the Chimney Sweeps Act forbade the apprenticeship of any child under the age of 10, and prohibited anyone under the age of 14 from being involved in the cleaning of chimneys. These regulations were largely ignored, as were those of the 1840 Chimney Sweeps Act (which raised the minimum age of apprenticeship to 16). Despite the government's best efforts, young children were still routinely forced to climb up inside the narrowest of chimneys to clean out the soot and any other detritus that had become lodged inside.

Campaigning writers brought the plight of the chimney-sweep boys to the public consciousness. In Charles Dickens's *Oliver Twist* (published in instalments between 1837 and 1839), young Oliver – a child born in the workhouse – is offered by the parish authorities to anyone willing to take him off their hands. As an incentive, whoever takes him will also be given £5. A chimney sweep (who is in debt) wants him – a workhouse child would be a skinny child, the perfect size for sending up chimneys. Dickens mentions that the sweep has "bruised three or four boys to death already". He also explains how master sweeps forced their apprentices to work harder: if a child seemed to have got stuck in the chimney, the master would light a fire in the grate, to force the "lazy" child to move faster. In reality, as in the novel, many children were killed by this brutal practice. (Oliver Twist is not given to the sweep, and ends up as an apprentice to an undertaker instead.)

By the 1860s, the practice of using children as chimney sweeps had still not been properly outlawed, and people who employed sweeps were continuing to turn a blind eye to the children's plight. In Charles Kingsley's fairytale *The Water Babies*, a young chimney sweep named Tom drowns while trying to escape from his cruel master. He comes back to life but lives underwater as a "water baby". In 1864, the year after Kingsley's campaigning story was published, a new Chimney Sweeps' Regulation Act was passed. Once again, it was seldom enforced. It was not until the Chimney Sweepers' Act of 1875 – and its insistence that it was the duty of the police to enforce it – that things started to change. The Act also required all chimney sweeps to be licensed.

> *Once upon a time there was a little chimney-sweep, and his name was Tom. That is a short name, and you have heard it before, so you will not have much trouble in remembering it. He lived in a great town in the North Country, where there were plenty of chimneys to sweep, and plenty of money for Tom to earn and his master to spend. He could not read nor write, and did not care to do either; and he never washed himself, for there was no water up the court where he lived. He had never been taught to say his prayers. He never had heard of God, or of Christ, except in words which you never have heard, and which it would*

*have been well if he had never heard. He cried half his time,
and laughed the other half.*

The Water Babies: A Fairytale for a Land Baby
by Charles Kingsley, 1863

THE SHREWSBURY CASE

The Society for the Prevention of Cruelty to Children (now the
NSPCC) was set up in 1884 by the Reverend Benjamin Waugh.
Other similar societies had been set up in the past, but this was the
first one to cater for the whole nation. It was controversial from the
beginning – not least when it highlighted abuse within a wealthy
family, known as "the Shrewsbury Case". The SPCC (as it was
then known) prosecuted a doctor and his wife from Shrewsbury,
Shropshire, for beating their daughter with a riding whip. Both
parents were found guilty of common assault. The SPCC put
forward the case that in such instances, the society itself should
be made the child's guardian, and that abused children should be
removed from their family and cared for in a refuge.

14

EVERYDAY LIFE

It is often difficult to understand what everyday life was really like in the Victorian age, because images that have come down to us, from literature and art, show such a stylised type of life, and usually focus on celebrities or criminals, rather than the average person. Victorian Britons lived at a time when everything was changing at a rapid pace, from the type of food that was available and the textiles used to make their clothes, to the latest major scientific and technological breakthroughs. By the end of Queen Victoria's reign, Britain and the lives of many British people had changed dramatically from how life had been in the Georgian era.

THE PENNY POST

Prior to 1840, the postal system in Britain was very expensive and confusing. The cost of posting a letter was calculated by the distance it was travelling and by the number of sheets of paper inside the envelope. It was usually the recipient who had to pay for the postage. Letters sent to and from the House of Commons and the House of Lords could be posted free of charge; the royal household could also send and receive letters for nothing.

In 1832, the campaigner Rowland Hill had published a campaigning pamphlet addressing the issue, *Post Office Reform: Its Importance and Practicability*. He suggested radical changes and introducing a much simpler and cheaper postal service. On 10 January 1840, the Penny Post was introduced, with a uniform fee (one penny) for all letters. Legislation was also passed to abolish free franking (which had benefitted only the wealthiest people, who could well afford to pay for their postage stamps). The new system was a huge success and dramatically increased the number of letters sent in Britain. Throughout 1839, more than 75 million letters were sent – just over a decade later, this had increased to nearly 350 million letters a year.

PILLAR BOXES

At the start of the Penny Post, Britain did not have post boxes. Letters were taken to a receiving house (the precursor of the post office) or collected by a bellman (who walked around at specific times of the day to collect any post that needed to be sent). Of course, it was only the most highly populated areas that had bellmen. The name came from the bell that the man rang as he walked to alert people to the fact that he was collecting in their road.

The British post box, or pillar box, was the idea of a novelist. Anthony Trollope (1815–82) is today best known for his novels, but he was never a fulltime writer. He worked for the post office as a surveyor's clerk, and even when his books became very successful, he kept on his day job. His work involved regular travelling overseas and he was impressed by the post boxes he saw in other European countries – so he proposed that Britain should have them too.

PILLAR BOX FACTS

- The name "pillar box" came about because of their early design, which was inspired by fluted Doric architectural pillars.
- The very first pillar boxes in the British Isles were the three installed on the island of Jersey, on the Channel Islands, in 1853. A short time later, another six were installed on the island of Guernsey.
- The Channel Island pillar boxes were such a success that by the end of the year they were starting to be introduced in the rest of Britain. There was no standard design at this date, and the appearance of a pillar box depended on local designers.
- Initially, most pillar boxes were green, in order to blend in with the local landscape. However, people complained that they couldn't find them, and so the red pillar box was introduced.

⚡ The first uniform for post-office employees was issued in the eighteenth century, but, although the service employed women as well as men, there was no woman's uniform until 1894. In that year, female employees were issued with standard waterproof capes and skirts.

⚡ Many early Victorian letters were "cross written", meaning that, to economize, the writer covered an entire sheet of very thin paper, then turned the paper sideways and wrote across their earlier words. A cross-written letter needed to be read both vertically and horizontally – and on both sides of each sheet of paper.

COUNTING THE POPULATION

In 1801, the very first census of the British population was carried out. It was a way of counting how many people lived in the country and it was decided that a new census would be taken every 10 years. The census of 1841 was the first to record the name of every person. In 1851, new categories were added, including age, occupation, place of birth and family relationships.

VICTORIAN CURRENCY

In Victoria's reign, the currency was made up of pounds, shillings and pence, or "L.S.D." These abbreviations derive from Latin:

L = *librae* (pounds)
S = *solidi* (shillings)
D = *denarii* (pence)

There were 12 pence (12d) in one shilling (1s).
A pound was made up of 20 shillings.
A shilling was known as a "bob".

Coins were composed of copper, bronze, silver and gold. The smallest Victorian coin was a farthing (a quarter of a penny). The other coins were:

- a halfpenny (ha'penny)
- twopence (tuppence)
- threepence (thruppence)
- a groat (4d coin)
- sixpence
- florin (2s)
- double florin (4s)
- half crown (2s 6d)
- crown (5s)
- half sovereign (worth 10s)
- sovereign (20s, i.e. £1)
- double sovereign (£2)
- five-pound coin

Bank notes were available in denominations of £5, £10, £20, £100, £200, £500 and £1,000.

Victorians still talked about the "guinea", even though that coin had not been made since 1813. It was still considered the gentleman's or artisan's rate of pay: for example, an artist would expect to be paid in guineas, whereas a tradesman would be paid in pounds. Paying an artist in pounds was considered an insult. Luxury goods were advertised as being sold in guineas. In order to pay in a currency that was no longer being produced, one guinea could be converted to £1 1s.

⇥ The modern-day symbol for £ comes from the the letter L written in Victorian cursive script.

VISITING ETIQUETTE

In middle- and upper-class society, the rules around "calling on" (or paying a visit to) someone were strictly governed and could be very confusing to outsiders. Rules differed according to how well one knew a person, according to the social rank or age of the visitor and the person being visited, and according to whether either party was in mourning. Calling cards were the equivalent of modern-day business cards. They were left, usually with the maid or butler, after the first visit if the recipient was "not at home" (or pretending not to be at home), and the obligation was then with the person who had received the card to pay a return visit within a certain number of days. When a face-to-face visit finally took place, it was expected that the visitor would stay for around 15 minutes. Overstaying one's welcome was a serious social faux pas.

CHURCH

In Victorian Britain, Protestant Christianity was the most widespread religion. People of other religions – including those of other Christian faiths – were still looked upon with suspicion. Society's rules expected everyone to attend church each Sunday unless ill ("illness" also included being in an advanced stage of pregnancy). Even those with little Christian belief attended church as a matter of etiquette. To not do so was considered scandalous. Churchgoers dressed in their finest clothes, known as "Sunday best"; men and boys had to remove their hats in church, whereas women and girls needed to keep their heads covered. In smaller towns and rural communities, church was often the best way to get to see one's neighbours and any newcomers. It was also a very good place for single people to meet each other.

⚑ When walking along a street or pavement, men were expected to walk on the outside of women; this was to ensure that if anyone got dirtied or splashed by the mud from passing traffic, it would be the man.

SMOKING

- Only men were expected to smoke. If a woman did so, it was considered scandalous or bohemian, depending on what type of society she lived in.
- Men were expected not to smoke in front of women.
- At dinner parties and social gatherings, a "smoking room" would often be set aside for men.
- Queen Victoria disapproved wholeheartedly of smoking. When her son the Prince of Wales – who was famous for his cigar-smoking habit – was invited to visit, she would instruct her staff to lock the doors of any room in which he might have been permitted to smoke.

The Queen did not know that her daughter Princess Louise was also a smoker.

- In the 1870s, St Pancras station in London made history when it opened its Gentlemen's and Ladies' Smoking Room. This was the first room in Europe where men and women were permitted to smoke together in public.

MOURNING CONVENTIONS

Mourning was a complicated business, and it was vitally important to get it right. The Victorian obsession with death and mourning increased exponentially after Prince Albert died and the Queen went into a state of mourning that she refused to leave for 40 years. She insisted that Albert's bedroom be turned into a living shrine, with the bedlinen changed every day as if he were still alive, and fresh flowers replenished regularly. She slept with a plaster cast of his hand beside her in bed.

Women's magazines gave regular mourning tips and specifics, such as what stage of mourning should be worn for each relative, no matter how distant, and for how long. Deep mourning meant wearing only black clothes, and certain materials and particular finishes to those materials were also specified. For a less close relative or for a later stage of mourning, sombre-coloured clothes, such as dark grey or purple could be worn, edged with black crepe. As black was one of the most expensive dyes, launderers and textile manufacturers made a fortune from the fashion for mourning, as did producers of black jet jewellery and hair accessories. It was considered bad luck to keep mourning clothes after the specified period of time ended, so wealthier families discarded their clothing until the next family death when a whole new set of mourning clothes needed to be acquired. Poorer families had no choice but to keep wearing the same outfits.

Homes were also given mourning outfits, with black crepe used to muffle the doorknocker, as well as being draped over picture frames and mirrors.

POST-MORTEM PHOTOGRAPHY

Post-mortem photography was a big industry in Victorian Britain. This new invention helped people to cope with their grief and gave them a permanent reminder of their loved one. When looking at a post-mortem photograph, it is sometimes not obvious who the dead person is, as they have been propped up as though still alive. Children were often laid out in bed, but many adults were dressed and placed in a chair as though simply sleeping before being photographed. As photography technology improved towards the end of the nineteenth century, photographers would often hand-tint a photograph to give pale cheeks a rosy glow. People's eyes could also be propped open to give the impression that the photograph had been taken while the deceased was still alive.

THE END OF THE VICTORIAN AGE

Queen Victoria died at Osborne House, on the Isle of Wight, on 22 January 1901. Her coffin was taken to London and then transported to St George's Chapel, Windsor, for her state funeral on 2 February. On the day of the funeral, the procession passed through the streets of Windsor, with the coffin on a gun carriage being drawn by the Royal Horse Artillery; but there was a problem with the carriage and the horses became unable to move it. Halfway through the procession, sailors from the Royal Navy took over the task from the horses and pulled the gun carriage with its coffin to the chapel. Following the funeral, the coffin lay in state for two days, before being buried in the family mausoleum at Frogmore, Windsor. Queen Victoria was buried next to her husband, Prince Albert.

Among the curiously mingled impressions left by to-day's great ceremony in London, that of the immense dignity and sincerity of the nation's mourning stands out most sharply. The funeral procession, although of great length, was extremely simple in character and, considered purely as a pageant, would have been comparatively unimpressive. Its greatness lay in the vast unison of a human feeling which it evoked and in its power to clothe what was probably the most representative crowd that London ever assembled in one grand garment of simple mourning. The scene of to-day will never be forgotten by those who regarded it.

Nothing could have been more worthy of an honoured monarch and nothing more creditable to her country. When one considers the emotional sympathy of the great crowd and all the massed effects of military pomp and royal dignity, of thousands of men stepping slowly to the measure of solemn music, of the mingling of pride and pathos, triumph and pity, grandeur and humility round the dust of one simple lonely woman – then, indeed, one may realise the significance of to-day's scene.

Manchester Guardian, 4 February 1901

OTHER TITLES IN THIS SERIES INCLUDE:

THE TUDOR TREASURY
A collection of fascinating facts and insights about the Tudor dynasty
Elizabeth Norton

ISBN: 9780233004334

Magna Carta and All That
A guide to the Magna Carta and life in England in 1215
Rod Green

ISBN: 9780233004648

THE AGINCOURT COMPANION
A guide to the legendary battle and warfare in the medieval world
Anne Curry

ISBN: 9780233004716